Lady Godiva

Lady Godiva

A Literary History of the Legend

DANIEL DONOGHUE

Blackwell
Publishing

350 Main Street, Malden, MA 02148-5018, USA
108 Cowley Road, Oxford OX4 1JF, UK
530 Swanston Street, Carlton South, Victoria 3053, Australia
Kurfürstendamm 57, 10707 Berlin, Germany

First published 2003 by Blackwell Publishing Ltd

Library of Congress Cataloging-in-Publication Data has been applied for.

ISBN 1–405–10046–X (hbk); ISBN 1–405–10047–8 (pbk)

A catalogue record for this title is available from the British Library.

Set in 10 on 12.5 pt Meridien
by Ace Filmsetting Ltd, Frome, Somerset
Printed and bound in the United Kingdom
by MPG Books, Bodmin, Cornwall

For further information on
Blackwell Publishing, visit our website:
http://www.blackwellpublishing.com

Contents

Acknowledgments

Tracing a reception history as wide-ranging as the Godiva legend is both exhilarating and daunting: exhilarating because of the opportunity to discover and rediscover the cultural record outside my area of specialization, and daunting because it is so vast. Because my project accompanies Lady Godiva as she ambles away from her home in the Middle Ages through the marketplace of various periods and disciplines, I am enormously indebted to colleagues who gave me the benefit of their advice in mapping out my early drafts. They include Christopher Cannon, Glenn Davis, Robin Fleming, Elizabeth Fowler, Katherine French, Scott Gordon, Joseph Harris, Christoph Irmscher, Margaret Kim, Rebecca Krug, Jeff Masten, Derek Pearsall, Jason Puskar, Allen Reddick, Alexandra Reid-Schwartz, Bryan Reynolds, Gustavo Secchi, and Jane Tolmie. To these I would add the anonymous readers, whose reports were as helpful as they were encouraging, and the many acquaintances who gave me leads on sources and who volunteered personal anecdotes. I gratefully acknowledge the help of Ronald Aquilla Clarke of the Herbert Art Gallery and Museum for his assistance with visual images and the local history of Coventry. I thank Andrew McNeillie of Blackwell for his initial interest in the project and generous encouragement. My thanks also for the comments and suggestions by participants when I delivered various iterations of my Godiva research at the ISAS Conference at Oxford, the Medieval Doctoral Conference at Harvard University, Smith College, the G. L. Brook Symposium at Manchester University, the University of Zurich, and the University of Connecticut. Finally I thank my wife Ann for making this and so much else possible.

Some material in this book is derived from my essay "Lady Godiva," in Donald Scragg and Carole Weinberg, eds., *Literary Appropriations of the Anglo-Saxons from the Thirteenth to the Twentieth Century* (Cambridge: Cambridge University Press, 2000). All lines from "Ariel" from *Ariel* by Sylvia Plath. Copyright © 1965 by Ted Hughes. Reprinted by permission of HarperCollins Publishers Inc. "Ariel" also reproduced from *Collected Works* by Sylvia Plath, by permission of Faber and Faber Ltd.

Illustrations

Abbreviations

ASC	*Anglo-Saxon Chronicle*, ed. and trans. Dorothy Whitelock, D. C. Douglas, and S. I. Tucker. New Brunswick: Rutgers University Press, 1961
Burbidge	F. Bliss Burbidge, *Old Coventry and Lady Godiva*. Birmingham: Cornish Brothers, 1952
Chronica Majora	Matthew Paris, *Chronica Majora* (ca. 1250), ed. H. L. Luard, Rolls Series, 7 vols. London: Longman, 1872–84
Clarke and Day	Ronald Aquilla Clarke and Patrick A. E. Day, *Lady Godiva: Images of a Legend in Art and Society*. Coventry: City of Coventry Leisure Services, 1982
DNB	Leslie Stephen and Sidney Lee, eds., *Dictionary of National Biography*, 22 vols. London: Humphrey Milford, 1917–22
EHD I	*English Historical Documents*, vol. i: *c.500–1042*, ed. Dorothy Whitelock, 2nd edn. London: Routledge, 1979
EHD II	*English Historical Documents*, vol. ii: *1042–1189*, ed. David C. Douglas and George W. Greenaway. New York: Oxford University Press, 1968
Ingram, REED	R. W. Ingram, *Coventry*, Records of Early English Drama. Toronto: Toronto University Press, 1981
John of Worcester	*The Chronicle of John of Worcester*, trans. Jennifer Bray and P. McGurk, ed. R. R. Darlington and P. McGurk, vol. ii. Oxford: Clarendon Press, 1995

Lancaster, *Godiva*   Joan C. Lancaster, *Godiva of Coventry*, Coventry
                           Papers, vol. i. Coventry: Coventry Corporation,
                           1967

OED   *Oxford English Dictionary*, 2nd edn. Oxford:
                           Clarendon Press, 1989

Map of Godiva's England, late eleventh century

Introduction

Everyone, it seems, has heard of Lady Godiva. To most people her name calls to mind an image of a naked woman on a horse. A smaller number are able to recall details of a story about Godiva's ride: that it took place in medieval Coventry, that she did it at the instigation of her husband in order to alleviate an oppressive tax, that the citizens were forbidden to look, that one man looked at her and was struck blind. A few pedants are aware that this voyeur is the origin of the phrase Peeping Tom. Still others with a vague recollection of the legend may assume that Godiva is folk-tale heroine rather than a flesh-and-blood woman from eleventh-century England. And many of those who have heard of the historical woman are surprised to learn how long after her death the enchanting story became attached to her name. The historical Godiva turns out to be an ordinary woman who lived through some of the most extraordinary decades of English history. Even if she never made a naked ride through Coventry, her unlegendary life makes a compelling story.

My interest in this topic began several years ago with the realization that the most famous individual from my period of expertise, Anglo-Saxon England, is not Alfred the Great or the Venerable Bede or any of the other worthies that spring to mind. No, the most famous, as far as name recognition is concerned, is Lady Godiva. It struck me as odd that my medievalist colleagues and I knew little about the historical woman and seemed indifferent to the legend that had overtaken her. She may be the most celebrated Anglo-Saxon for everyone else, but Anglo-Saxonists generally ignore her. The source of Godiva's fame has little to do with what we spend our time researching. If she merits a mention in our publications at all, it is with a raised eyebrow or a passing witticism before returning to the more serious matters at hand. There is something too tawdry about the story of the ride to make it a suitable topic for research. Besides, we know it most likely never happened.

Gradually, however, I was drawn to the paradox that those of us who have the most to say about Lady Godiva have been conspicuously silent, especially because the legend (however spurious) opens an opportunity to draw a wider audience into the culture of early medieval England. At first, however, my ambitions were limited to a personal quest to become acquainted with Godgifu of Mercia and the legend of the ride. Then in the mid-1990s, after I assumed the duties as Chair of Harvard's History and Literature undergraduate program, I decided to pursue it as a full-fledged interdisciplinary project consistent with the pedagogic goals of the program. My journey with Godiva has indeed been interdisciplinary. We have moved at a brisk canter away from my home base in medieval literature through an imposing number of other disciplines from every period up to the present day. Another motivation for the project, which became apparent only after it was underway, is that despite Lady Godiva's name recognition, the traditional story of the ride is fading from collective memory. All the more reason, it seemed, for a retrospective survey.

Two themes unite the chapters of this book. They are the themes that inform every version of Godiva's ride from its first appearance in the thirteenth century to the present day. One is the nostalgic idealization of the Middle Ages now known as medievalism. When J. R. R. Tolkien and J. K. Rowling fantasize a world for their fiction, for example, the centuries that separate them from the medieval past open up a creative space for their literary imaginations, unencumbered by a still active memory. The Middle Ages are distant yet still accessible. What is remarkable in Godiva's case is that the fictional idealization arose less than two centuries after she died, yet her world was already considered remote enough that it could be imaginatively reconstructed. The second theme concerns the dynamics of the voyeuristic gaze – the surreptitious viewing of an eroticized body on display. The legend dramatizes the taboo associated with voyeurism, but it is typically invoked only to be circumvented. It also celebrates Godiva's physical beauty and the pleasures of the gaze, but in ways that strive to maintain social respectability. It justifies the scandal of her deed by imputing a self-sacrificing motive. It opens up a complex array of contiguous issues, such as the relation between the private and public, guilt and shame, desire, taboo, honor, scapegoating, and the gendering of the gaze. Each telling or re-enactment of Godiva's ride not only invites a viewing of a body, but also constructs the framework for that viewing. The dynamics of the gaze fall into three general categories. First, written narratives direct the reader to imagine Godiva's naked body even while they forbid that view to Coventry's residents. The second perspective is an extension of the first, in which a specified voyeur within the narrative (the Peeping Tom) is punished as a scapegoat. The third is on display not in written texts but during re-enactments of the ride, where the crowds are offered a spectacle that disrupts the conventional distinctions between public and private viewing.

Since beginning this project I have conducted informal surveys of my students and acquaintances about who they think Godiva was, and where and when she lived. The younger informants quite often associate her name merely with the image of a naked woman on a horse (hence my conviction that the full narrative is becoming a fading memory). Older informants are the ones most likely to recall details of the traditional narrative and to place her in medieval Coventry. Of those who have only a vague recollection of the story, a surprising number locate her elsewhere in Europe, such as seventeenth-century France. The inclination to place her in the *ancien régime* and the like owes something to her name, which in its current pronunciation sounds as though it belongs to a Romance language. What started off as an ordinary Old English name (Godgifu) fell out of fashion so completely after 1100 that by the end of the Middle Ages even English speakers had to guess at the pronunciation, and the guesswork led to the now familiar "Godiva." The honorific "Lady" was an even later (and anachronistic) addition.

The free-floating name is only one indication that in the popular imagination Godiva has become unmoored from her historical context. Neither King Arthur, Joan of Arc, nor Robin Hood, to pick three comparable legendary figures with roots in medieval Europe, has suffered as much dislocation. In Godiva's case it is compounded by the general perception of the early Middle Ages as too unexciting, too undecadent for a gesture as flamboyant as her naked ride is taken to be. As it turns out, this view is a half-truth: Lady Godiva didn't make such a ride in eleventh-century England, but it has nothing to do with the decadence of the period when she lived.

Suspended as she is between the never-never land of fairy tales and a remote historical period, Lady Godiva as a subject for study can be hard to keep in focus. It requires a double perspective. If today we knew only the historical Godgifu, her life's story might fill out a scholarly article.

But because the legend of the ride has overtaken her and inspired so many different versions, a survey like this cannot hope to be comprehensive. This book's organization follows what might be called the lady's two bodies: on the one hand, the historical woman whose remains were buried in the monastery she endowed in Coventry; and on the other the fictionalized body on display, famously naked. The chapters trace the legend from its earliest appearance in the thirteenth century through its dissemination up to today. But before the chronological survey it summarizes what can be gathered from the scant sources about the historical Godiva, who lived in the last decades of Anglo-Saxon England. As the wife of an earl she moved in the highest social and political circles of the kingdom during turbulent times, yet we know few details about her life. Such reticence in the historical record is not unusual, since the sources from the time pay more attention to the men in power (and when haven't they?). Comparatively little is recorded about women in eleventh-century England and elsewhere. But enough survives concerning Godiva to give a better glimpse than for most of her contemporaries: we know her husband and children, the town where they lived, her peers, her landholding, her generosity to religious foundations, and her piety. We know that she died in 1067 and where she was buried. But we do not know her parents or when or where she was born, and there is much more we can never recover.

The earliest extant account of the ride through Coventry does not appear for about 150 years after Godiva's death, when chroniclers from the monastery of St. Albans insert a surprisingly detailed narrative into their histories. From the start it marks Godiva's act as heroic and legitimizes the voyeuristic gaze, a perspective that her husband and the narrator (the two sources of authority) encourage the reader/viewer to adopt. The second chapter introduces the legend and charts its rapid dissemination. It also points out how the story depends on assumptions about the legal and economic status of women in post-Conquest England that would not apply to the historical Godiva. Most significantly, Godiva – not her husband – held Coventry from the king and thus would have no need to plead with him to lower the citizens' taxes. It was not until the arrival of Norman legal conventions in 1066 that the rights of married women like Godiva to possess property were curtailed in ways that would fit the earliest narrative's plot.

The third chapter takes up the legend from the later Middle Ages into the eighteenth century, when Godiva evolves from a local celebrity to a national hero. It begins by examining Godiva processions in Coventry, which from the seventeenth century have ritually re-enacted a number of events linked by history or legend to the town. By the end of the Middle Ages Coventry was one of the largest urban centers in England, and its religious pageants and processions were a point of civic pride. Some of these elements were taken over into the more secularized processions after the Reformation, which continued to stage the townspeople's sense of civic identity, but they also contained the seeds for religious parody in elevating Godiva's undivine body for public veneration. The processions proved to be tremendously popular, attracting tens of thousands of spectators in the nineteenth century. The chapter also discusses the spread of the legend in poetry and chronicles.

The fourth chapter traces the strange development of Peeping Tom, who slinks in several centuries after the earliest versions of the Godiva legend. In the early modern period an edict forbidding the town's citizens to gaze on Godiva during her ride is added to the legend. Almost immediately this change in plot provokes the invention of a character who defies the edict and is consequently, mysteriously punished with blindness or death. His voyeuristic role has proved so durable because its combination of transgression and wish-fulfillment has found deep resonances in modern Western culture.

Medievalism of all kinds enjoyed a heyday in the Victorian period, as the fifth chapter shows, but the attention to Godiva is especially impressive: dozens of paintings, sculptures, poems, novels, drama, opera, and more. Tennyson's famous poem (in the 1842 volume that launched his career) is perhaps a watershed moment in the popularization and interpretation of the legend. Part of its appeal derives from the way it lays out binary opposites, which permit readers to dwell on the more respectable element of each pair to reinforce public ideals of heroism, self-sacrifice, and duty. With guilt consigned to Peeping Tom and Godiva's shame aesthetically transformed, the reader assumes a voyeuristic perspective with impunity. Yet the eroticism still provides the legend with its energy. Nineteenth-century women such as Anna Jameson and even Queen Victoria herself found ways to appropriate the legend for their public personas by invoking Godiva as an example of self-sacrifice for the common good. The high seriousness which characterizes the Victorian reception made Godiva a target for parodies in many genres: poems, musicals, plays, and the Coventry procession itself.

In the twentieth century the sense of narrative and historical grounding which the legend enjoyed in the Victorian period becomes more attenuated. It is as though Godiva's context has been left behind with her clothes, and increasingly she circulates as a cultural icon, though one with world-wide currency. In North America at least she is thought to be vaguely European, vaguely pre-modern. What is left of the older narrative has undergone a bifurcation, with an innocently erotic strand epitomized by the globally advertised logo of Godiva Chocolatier. The other strand explores violence and control implicit in the gaze, as with Michael Powell's 1960 film *Peeping Tom*. In a remarkable contrast to Powell, Sylvia Plath's 1962 poem "Ariel" recasts the basic terms of the legend to make Godiva no longer a vulnerable object of the gaze but an independent, self-defining subject.

While the legend of Lady Godiva appeared with mysterious sudden-ness in the thirteenth century, it has entered the twenty-first century in a precarious state. She may be the best-known Anglo-Saxon, but the famous deed attributed to her has largely been forgotten. For centuries the story of her ride was an astonishingly productive instance of medievalism, and now it seems increasingly trivialized. Why should so many details about it be fading from memory today? The answer, I suggest, is connected with the dominance of cinema, by which I do not mean any particular film or even the aggregate of all films, but rather the medium itself. Film criticism has shown that the medium functions through the imposition of the same male gaze articulated by the Godiva legend. Now that cinema has become ubiquitous, the gaze does not need a legend to convey those values; they are conveyed indirectly. Or to adjust Marshall McLuhan's formula, the medium is the legend. Cin-ema is now doing much of the cultural work that the traditional Godiva legend was doing (on a more modest scale) for centuries. It is almost as though Lady Godiva's oxygen has been sucked away as the film indus-try rushes past, leaving her an unnoticed casualty of larger cultural forces. However, the history of the legend cannot be reduced to a simple rise and decline, because even if the fuller narrative is disappearing from view, the name and image of Godiva remain remarkably current. Who knows what the future holds? If everyone has heard of Lady Godiva, then perhaps we haven't heard the last of her.

Chapter 1

Godgifu of Mercia

Even though Lady Godiva's name enjoys world-wide recognition to-day, the biographical details of the medieval woman remain obscure. Godgifu, as she was known to her contemporaries, lived during a period of extraordinary political turmoil in England. If she reached her mid-fifties when she died in 1067, her lifetime would have spanned nine different kings of England drawn from four different ruling families.[1] Nothing is known about Godgifu's parents, though one plausible tradition locates her family in the region near Nottingham and Lincoln, where her largest estates lay. For most of her adult life she was married to Leofric, the earl of Mercia, who was one of England's most influential political players. As wife and husband they controlled an enormous amount of wealth in estates scattered across the Midlands. A significant proportion, including Coventry, was held by Godgifu alone, who, according to Anglo-Saxon law, could possess property independently of her husband. As a couple she and Leofric jointly endowed a number of religious institutions, which clerics gratefully acknowledge in writing, thus ensuring that later generations knew of their generosity. But many other details of their life, which did not gain the attention of literate clerics, have gone unrecorded. The family fortunes reached a pinnacle in 1066 when Godgifu's granddaughter became the last queen of Anglo-Saxon England. Even apart from the famous ride, Godgifu's biography is worth attending to because she led a privileged life in interesting times.

As familiar as the name "Godiva" may be today, the current pronunciation and spelling disguise its Anglo-Saxon roots so that many people assume (if pressed) that it derives from a Romance language. It does not strike the eye or ear the same way as Edith or Æthelflæd. Yet in pre-Conquest England, the name God-gifu was a typical compound meaning "good gift," pronounced with the primary accent on the first syllable (*goad*-yivu). It was common enough, in fact, that in one notable instance the name was used derisively as an all-too-typical Anglo-Saxon appellation (like John and Jane Doe or, perhaps more pointedly, Bruce and Sheila for Australians). Early chronicles tell the story that around the year 1100 some Norman nobles from a rival faction mocked King Henry I and his new wife Matilda by calling them Godric and Godgifu, not because of ethnicity (Henry's father was William the Conqueror and Matilda was descended from both English and Scottish royal lines), but because their conduct was considered too "common," and to the Anglo-Normans commoners were synonymous with Anglo-Saxons.[2] Hence the quaint names. Such contempt can only be bred by familiarity. The name Godgifu eventually fell out of fashion as the use of the older English compounds increasingly gave way to names derived from French (for example, Eleanor) and the Latin Bible (for example, Elizabeth). At some point after 1100 the accent shifted to the second syllable. The older pronunciation was long forgotten by the later Middle Ages, when the name Godgifu was encountered only as a fossilized form in written records and under a variety of spellings (such as Godgyva, Godifa, Goditha, Godeva, etc.). Even in Coventry, where she continued to be revered, the name's lack of currency by 1495 gave rise to a folk etymology that transformed it to "Goode Eve." Not surprisingly, the history of Godgifu's name mimics the reputation of the woman: what started off as an unremarkable Old English word has been glamorized into something that Godgifu herself would find hard to recognize.

Drawing from a variety of sources, this chapter gives an overview of Godgifu's life and times. It begins with the political and social world of late Anglo-Saxon England, with special attention to Leofric's important role in the affairs of the kingdom. It then discusses the scope of action available to a high-ranking woman like Godgifu. Finally, infusing history with speculation, it offers a biographical sketch of Godgifu of Coventry.

Godgifu's England

Even though the year of Godgifu's birth is unknown, it quite possibly fell toward the end of the long reign of King Æthelred (979–1016), who came to power as a young teenager after his supporters murdered his half-brother, King Edward the Martyr. If Æthelred's reign began unpropitiously, it ended disastrously, and during the intervening years England was plagued by treason within its borders and Viking attacks from the sea. Æthelred pursued a policy of paying tribute to stave off the Vikings, which was somewhat effective in forestalling attacks, but by 1040 he and his successors had paid out over £250,000. However ineffective in the long run, paying tribute must have seemed like a reasonable policy to the king and his advisors, because England's coastline was far too extensive for permanent defense against armies as formidable and mobile as the sea-borne Vikings.

The popular reputation of Æthelred through the ages has been ungenerous, to say the least. Even today in England he is commonly remembered as a feeble ruler; Sir Frank Stenton calls him "a king of singular incompetence."[3] His reputation persists in part because of a nickname that dates from the Middle Ages, Æthelred the Unready. It seems ludicrous for anyone, much less a king, but in Old English "unready" meant something even more damning than what it means today. The Old English elements play on the words that make up *Æthel-ræd*, a compound that literally means "noble counsel." The possibility of using *ræd* to make a play on its opposite, *un-ræd*, "ill counsel" or "folly," was too attractive to pass up. The resulting oxymoron ("noble-foolish counsel") directs an unsubtle criticism of the king's unhappy political and military policies.[4]

The low point of Æthelred's career came between 1013 and 1014, when he was chased from England during the invasion by the king of Denmark, Swein Forkbeard. After Swein's sudden death in 1014 the English nobility allowed Æthelred to return (in the words of the *Anglo-Saxon Chronicle*) "if he would govern them more justly than he did before."[5] Æthelred died, apparently of natural causes, in 1016, during the invasion by Swein's son Cnut. Æthelred's son Edmund Ironside then became king, but after more defeats on the battlefield he too died later that year, which left the throne open for Cnut. While the anonymous writers of the *Chronicle* direct oblique criticisms at Æthelred's policies (including references to his poor counsel or *ræd*), they also castigate the treason of many members of the ruling class in England. Other contemporary observers see the social decline continue even during Cnut's comparatively stable reign (1016–35). In a famous homily first written during Æthelred's reign but revised and recirculated during Cnut's, the bishop and law-writer Wulfstan itemizes the many ways the entire population of England has sunk to the most heinous crimes of murder, rape, and illicit slavery. He saves his harshest denunciations, however, for the widespread treachery he witnessed in England.[6] Later, during the reign of Edward the Confessor (1042–66), the ruling classes continued to be embroiled in treacherous murders, mutilations, dispossessions, repudiated marriages, exile, and civil war. By the year of Edward's death in 1066, the throne of England had become the object of foreign invasions and intrigue that embroiled the ruling families of England, Normandy, and Denmark. William's victory at Hastings was only the final maneuver in a high-stakes international political game that had been underway for decades.

Against all appearances to the contrary, however, England had not slipped entirely into chaos over the course of Godgifu's lifetime. Much of the local and day-to-day workings of society continued despite the upheavals at the top. England remained a wealthy kingdom, with a well-organized system of currency and tax-collection. It was famous for the quality of its metalwork and needlework. Its monasteries maintained a high level of scholarship and art, and it developed a tradition of vernacular literature unmatched in continental Europe. Its comparative wealth and cultural sophistication made England an attractive prize for the ambitions of men like Cnut and William of Normandy.

When Cnut came to the throne in 1016 he joined England to an extensive Scandinavian empire and imposed order by reconstituting the highest level of the aristocracy with a few hand-picked men who were given the new title of "earl" (replacing "ealdorman"). Cnut's reformation signaled the end of a centuries-long tradition of government. Until the end of the tenth century the ruling classes of England were held together by a complex web of landholding and kinship. Where links through blood or marriage did not exist, ritualistic ties of kinship were sealed by fosterage and the sponsorship of godparents. One of the advantages of such an arrangement was that it discouraged revolt or large-scale disputes. The chances were very good that insurrection would result in the loss of land and involve warfare against one's kin The thick network of ties by blood, marriage, fosterage, and other rituals was a powerful cohesive force in Anglo-Saxon society, and included almost everyone of consequence. The ties acted as a horizontal network extending out from the vertical hierarchies inevitably found in such a society, a network which protected legal rights and maintained peace. At least it did so until the reign of Æthelred, when widespread corruption jeopardized it for everyone.

As a foreign-born king, however, Cnut deliberately limited his innovations. In seeking public acceptance as the legitimate successor to Alfred the Great and the royal line of the West Saxons, he made a conspicuous display of his support for traditional Anglo-Saxon laws and institutions, including the Church. He also married Æthelred's widow, Emma. But his elimination of the old office of ealdorman in favor of the new office of earl had far-reaching consequences. The new earls were no longer born into a network of family and ritualistic alliances that had bound the older aristocracy to one another and to the king. Cnut promoted men of demonstrated loyalty and ability, no matter what their family background. Not long after 1016 the leading members of the older dominant families were killed or exiled, and their offices and land were arrogated by Cnut's three new earls. The newcomers were Godwine of Wessex, Siward of Northumbria, and Leofric of Mercia, whose families grew to wield extraordinary power for about fifty years. Until William was crowned in 1066 all high-stakes political intrigue involved England's most powerful earls, not to mention Denmark's and Normandy's ruling families, and England's ancient royal family of Wessex.

Leofric, whose father was an ealdorman under the old regime, came from a more distinguished family than Godwine or Siward, but he became an earl only after Cnut executed his brother Northman, who had been ealdorman up to that point. It seems that Leofric was able to accept his brother's death without demur, because he remained loyal to Cnut and adroit enough as an earl to remain in power for forty years without the supportive network that previous generations of Anglo-Saxon aristocracy had cultivated. Earl Godwine, whose father was a commoner, was to prove even more successful because of his ambition and resourcefulness. Eventually, the landed wealth of the Godwine family outstripped that of Edward the Confessor, and upon the king's death in 1066 the family's greatest ambition was realized when Godwine's son Harold was crowned king for a short but eventful reign.[7] Earl Siward, who probably arrived in England as a follower of Cnut, has been described as "not a statesman, but a Danish warrior of a primitive type."[8] At first his earldom extended over only the part of Northumbria known as Deira, but for twenty years until his death in 1055 he dominated all of the region and is best remembered today for his defeat of Macbeth, king of the Scots, in 1054. Between the time of Cnut's death in 1035 and William's conquest, royal policy and the accession of Harold Harefoot (1035–40), Harthacnut (1040–2), and Edward the Confessor (1042–66) to the throne depended on the cooperation and approval of the three families (or two of them allied against the third). The danger of placing so much power in the hands of a few rival families is evident in the number of insurrections and exiles in the last fifteen years of Edward's reign, which led directly to the political instability that gave both Harold Godwineson and William of Normandy their chance after Edward's death in January 1066.

Leofric of Mercia

Early chronicles rarely associate the kingdom's turmoil with Leofric. From 1017 to his death in 1057 he grew to become one of the most powerful men in England and had the political shrewdness and good fortune to expand his family's power in the turmoil of these years. His earldom, Mercia, had once been an independent kingdom, until the ninth century when it was absorbed into the West Saxon dynasty. Its geographical position in the center of the island and adjacent to Wales made it crucial in keeping the larger kingdom of England intact. Despite its geopolitical importance its borders were remarkably elastic. Between 1017 and 1066 the earldom of Mercia expanded and shrank as Cnut and later kings assigned territories traditionally taken up by Mercia, Northumbria, East Anglia, and Wessex to different arrays of earls.[9]

Most of the early references to both Godgifu and Leofric are in chronicles under his *obit* in 1057, which single out his virtues as a statesman. One version of the *Anglo-Saxon Chronicle*, for example, speaks of Leofric as "very wise in divine and worldly matters, which benefited all his people."[10] Writing in the early twelfth century, John of Worcester calls him "a man of excellent memory," and continues, "The wisdom of this earl during his lifetime was of great advantage to the kings and all the people of the English." The same chronicle, referring to his appointment as earl in 1017 after Cnut ordered the execution of his brother, says that "afterwards the king held him in great affection."[11] There is little reason to doubt Leofric's loyalty to Cnut, but the details of his forty years as earl remain so sketchy that it is hard to judge. It is as if Leofric's wisdom consisted of staying out of the kind of trouble that made it into chronicle entries. His name surfaces in 1035, on the occasion of Cnut's death, when he is mentioned as a leader in the alliance to elect Harold Harefoot to the regency of England in a power-sharing arrangement with Harold's half-brother Harthacnut. Harthacnut was already king of Denmark, where he had to remain for three years because of a military threat from Norway.[12] Upon assuming the throne after Harold's death Harthacnut ordered Leofric, along with several other earls, to lead a punitive raid in 1041 against the town of Worcester, whose citizens had not only refused to pay the national tax he had imposed but had murdered the two men sent to collect it. Upon the approach of the army the citizens fled to an island, and after ravaging the town for five days the army set it afire and returned "with great booty," which slaked Harthacnut's anger.[13]

In 1043, after Harthacnut's sudden death, the three earls accompanied the newly crowned Edward the Confessor in a surprise raid against his mother Emma, the former queen who still controlled the royal treasury in Winchester. There was no love lost between mother and son because Emma had repudiated her children by Æthelred in favor of her children by Cnut. Edward ordered the earls to take "from his mother whatever gold, silver, gems, stones, or other precious objects she had, because, both before he became king and after, she had given him less than he wanted, and had been extremely harsh to him."[14] In 1047 and 1048 the king of Denmark asked Edward for ships to help in his war against Norway, and Earl Godwine urged the king to send "at least fifty ships" on each occasion. But "Earl Leofric and all the people" opposed it each time and won the king's ear.[15]

In 1051 Leofric was successful in counseling against a civil war that would have pitted one half of England against the other over a trivial dispute involving King Edward's brother-in-law. An army led by Godwine and his sons Swein and Harold were threatening the king, who was terrified and in great anguish (*perterritus, et in angore magno constitutus*) until he learned that the armies of Earls Leofric, Siward, and Ralph were approaching. Because the highest ranks of English society were ranged on each side, "it appeared to Earl Leofric and to certain others a great folly (*magnum uidebatur insilium*) that they should embark on a war with their compatriots." The episode ended peacefully, with Godwine and his family going into exile to Flanders. The next year they forced their way back into England, and once again cooler heads on both sides counseled a peaceful resolution. Godwine's family was restored to its former positions, and many of Edward's Norman favorites were exiled, including two whom Leofric allowed to escape through his territories on their way to find refuge in Scotland.[16] E. A. Freeman, the great nineteenth-century historian, elevates Leofric to an object lesson for Victorian England: "All that we know of the good old Earl of the Mercians leads us to look on him as a man who was quite capable of sacrificing the interests and passions of himself or his family to the general welfare of his country."[17]

There is yet another side to Leofric's career. The same chronicle that praises him for his wisdom lists an impressive number of benefactions to religious foundations, although most of these are linked to Godgifu as well. Along with the monastery they founded at Coventry, it lists seven other foundations that they enriched.[18] In addition to his benefactions, his piety is memorialized in two literary works. The first, a little-known Old English text copied not long after Leofric's death in 1057, describes four visions or miracles that he witnessed. The first begins with Leofric transported to heaven, where he looks over a crowd dressed in snow-white clothing, who receive the blessing of St. Paul at the end of a mass. In the second, Leofric's habit of praying through the night is rewarded by God one night after the locked doors of a church miraculously open and he finds himself wearing priestly vestments, including a shining green chasuble. On another evening when he goes to pray at the same church the inside is miraculously illuminated with a bright light. The fourth takes place in St. Clement's church, Sandwich, while King Edward is waiting there with a fleet (possibly 1045 or 1049). While hearing mass, Leofric sees a disembodied hand moving, as if it were blessing him. Leofric's vision ends, "A fortnight before his death he predicted the day that he had to go to his long-standing home in Coventry, where he lies; and it all happened as he said."[19]

The second text survives in a beautifully illuminated Anglo-Norman manuscript which was apparently the presentation copy of *The History of Saint Edward the King* for Eleanor of Provence, queen of Henry III. The poem may have been composed as early as 1235, but the manuscript was executed ca. 1250–60. The verses tell how Leofric and Godgifu, famous for their piety, join the king for a private mass in the old monastery of St. Peter at Westminster, during which they witness a miracle of the host. When the priest raises the host toward Edward its appearance is transformed from bread to the Infant Jesus, who blesses Edward. Afterwards the king swears Leofric to silence, but instead he returns to Worcester and confides in a priest, who puts the story in writing so that after Leofric's death the miracle can be revealed. In the manuscript an illustration shows a priest holding up a child, while King Edward stands with upraised arms and Leofric kneels. The head of a woman is visible in the background, partially blocked by the other figures. She must be Godgifu.[20]

The historical Leofric had a peculiarly ambivalent relationship with the clergy of Worcester. Besides the punitive raid on the town which he helped lead for King Harthacnut in 1041, he was also involved in legal disputes that deprived the Worcester abbey and cathedral of land.[21] Yet the two chronicles that are fullest in their praise and the two miracle texts were either written in Worcester or have other ties there (not Coventry, as might be expected). He and Godgifu also endowed the Worcester monastery with lands, but retained at least one of the disputed properties. These contradictory attributes (that he was rapacious, that he was saintly) do not have to be contemporary; they might point to a change of heart, where at some stage in his life he made pious amends for his earlier excesses and in turn was memorialized by the grateful clergy of Worcester. Because Leofric's father, Leofwine, was ealdorman of the region known as Hwicce, which is coextensive with the Worcester diocese, his involvement in land disputes there is not surprising, nor should one assume that the clergy's claims were always on the right side of the law.[22]

Aristocratic Women

Godgifu's position as the wife of the earl of Mercia gave her an important stake in the politics of England, and though the historical records reveal nothing of her views it would be misleading to interpret this silence as indifference. By the same token it would be just as misleading to accept the impressively documented story of her naked ride through Coventry as historically accurate. Between the scant historical record and the overblown legend, what can we learn about the historical Godgifu?

Her marriage to Leofric (some time before 1035) would have been negotiated in stages between their respective families. After the terms were settled, Leofric's pledge of betrothal was accompanied by gifts to her. She had the right to refuse his suit. The laws of Cnut (1020–3) explicitly prohibit forced marriages: "neither a widow nor a maiden is ever to be forced to marry a man whom she herself dislikes."[23] By the same token, Godgifu's orally declared assent to the proposal was a binding legal commitment because, as an Old English gnomic verse has it, "A woman must keep her pledge with a man."[24] The day after Godgifu was led to his house and their marriage was consummated, he presented her with a substantial "morning-gift." As a wife she would have control over the household goods, the dowry, the betrothal gift, and morning-gift. At this level of society, the gifts were not mere tokens; they could include large estates, gold, and expensive jewelry. The marriage negotiations would also specify what property Godgifu would be entitled to if she survived Leofric. As long as she remained unmarried in her parents' home a woman had little or no legal rights over the family property, but as a wife she could assume control over a substantial amount. Thus even though her marriage was arranged, and even though she had the right to refuse, Godgifu had compelling incentives for accepting such a match. Religious ceremony played a secondary role at this time, because marriage was considered primarily a secular contract between families. A short text "Concerning the Betrothal of a Woman" states, "At the marriage there should by rights be a priest, who shall unite them together with God's blessing in all prosperity," and such blessings survive from this period.[25] But the priest did not officiate over the vows of a marriage ceremony as clergy do today.

From our vantage point it may seem curious that Anglo-Saxon society did not confer a special title on the wife of an earl, but the absence simply reflects the political fact that only the husband held the office. Post-Conquest writers in Latin regularly bestow on Godgifu the anachronistic title "countess" as the feminine equivalent of Leofric's "count," but Old English writers did not have that option. In one charter the couple is identified as *Leofric eorl and Godgife þæs eorles wif*, "Earl Leofric and the earl's wife Godgifu." In another they are *Leofric eorl and his gebedda*, "Earl Leofric and his bed-partner," which may have sounded less indelicate to Anglo-Saxon ears than its sexual bluntness seems today.[26] Although the Old English word "lady" was available, at this time it was reserved as an honorific title for the queen alone. (The "Lady Godiva" familiar today was invented many centuries later.) It would be wrong to read the lack of honorific titles simply as a sign of her invisibility (although to be sure she was less visible in public affairs than her husband). Americans today, for example, have a similar problem with the president's spouse. Aside from "Wife of the President," the only option seems to be "First Lady," which sounds anachronistic and even trivializing in its quaintness. And to American sensibilities at least, the prospect of a "First Lord," when the time comes, makes the Anglo-Saxon "bed-partner" seem preferable in its unpretentiousness. Because Godgifu had considerable wealth independent of Leofric, as will be shown below, her own standing in society did not depend on a title derived from her husband.

A variety of evidence suggests that married women (and widows) in pre-Conquest England enjoyed rights to hold and dispose of land independently of their husbands and sons. A charter contemporary with Godgifu and Leofric, for example, dramatically illustrates this point by describing a legal transaction in Herefordshire. It begins with a son appearing in court to claim some land that belonged to his mother. She was not present at the time so the court appointed three thanes immediately to seek her out. On learning of her son's intention the mother grew furious and ensured that he would never inherit any of her possessions, even after her death. Before the three thanes as witnesses she declared, "Here sits my kinswoman Leofflæd, to whom I grant after my death my land and my gold, and my clothing and my raiment, and everything that I possess." When the thanes reported back, the court, which included Leofric's brother Edwin, promptly affirmed her new, orally declared will.[27] This vignette suggests considerable scope of action available for women of means. It shows a woman confident in her ability to use a court of law to assert her rights of ownership. It also suggests that there was no legal obstacle to a woman like Godgifu making a will that allocates land and goods in ways that work against primogeniture.

Other kinds of evidence can suggest the potential scope of action for women as landholders. A significant number of place-names from Anglo-Saxon England are derived from women's names. "Kenilworth" in Warwickshire, for example, derives from the name "Cynehild" and an Old English word for farm, *worþ.*[28] While women's names may have become associated with a settlement or a geographical feature for a variety of reasons, the simplest explanation is that they derive from a woman who happened to possess the land at an early date. More evidence about Godgifu and other women as landholders emerges from the Domesday Book, which William the Conqueror commissioned at Christmas of 1085 to provide an accounting of the extent of his vast holdings in England. "It is a record without parallel," according to one summary, and reflects the urgency "of a great king to obtain the fullest possible information about the kingdom he had won."[29] The *Anglo-Saxon Chronicle* takes a more jaundiced view: "So very narrowly did [William] have [England] investigated that there was no single hide nor virgate of land, nor one ox nor one cow nor one pig which was there left out, and not put down in his record; and all these records were brought to him afterwards."[30] Commissioners were sent to each shire, and among the questions they asked were the name of the landholder in 1066 and at the time of the inquiry, 1086. For reasons that have to do with simplifying the transfer of title, Domesday under-reports the amount of land possessed by married women. Much of the land that was held by a wife, even dowry, was listed under the possessions of her husband for both 1066 and 1086. Thus a relatively small number of women landholders appear in the Domesday Book, but a substantial amount of property is concentrated among a small number of widows in 1066. Godgifu's landholdings are discussed below. Two of the wealthiest individuals from 1066 are Gytha, the widow of Earl Godwine, and Eadgifu the Fair (or Edith Swansneck), who was the "handfast" or common-law wife of Harold.[31] By 1086 less land is listed under the control of women, largely because William had redistributed it to his followers as a reward for their role in the Conquest.

The most remarkable example of a woman's capacity to act independently in Anglo-Saxon England is that of Æthelflæd, known to her contemporaries as the "Lady of the Mercians." As the wife of the ealdorman of Mercia a century before Godgifu, her position was in many respects similar, although Æthelflæd was the daughter of a famous king, Alfred the Great.[32] Something of the uniqueness of her status is indicated in a charter from about 904 confirming the lease of lands to Æthelflæd and her husband Æthelred, which refers to the couple as "lords of the Mercians."[33] In this case the term "lords" suggests an equivalence between lord and lady. But even conferring the official title of "lady" was itself unusual.

Until the early ninth century Mercia had been an independent kingdom, powerful enough at times to subjugate other neighboring kingdoms. Because her husband Æthelred was ill for some years before his death, Æthelflæd assumed effective control of Mercia even before his death in 911.[34] Between 910 and 915 she oversaw the construction of ten fortresses as part of an ambitious program to consolidate Mercia and protect it from the Viking armies of that time. She also sent a punitive expedition against the Welsh in 916, and expanded her territory against the Vikings by gaining control of Derby and Leicester and receiving allegiance from the city of York. In all of these activities she acted as co-regent with her brother Edward the Elder, who had succeeded their father Alfred as king of Wessex. It was not until after Æthelflæd's death in 918 that King Edward assumed more direct control of Mercia, which thereafter was a region held by a subordinate (whether ealdorman or earl) under the kings from the West Saxon royal family.

Godgifu of Mercia

While Æthelflæd's career is famously exceptional, Godgifu exercised considerable legal and economic independence when, for example, she made donations to religious foundations. Medieval chroniclers are consistent in characterizing her as noble, generous, pious, and dedicated to the Blessed Virgin. John of Worcester, for example, calls her "the noble Countess Godgifu, a worshipper of God and devout lover of St. Mary ever-virgin."[35] Her name is first linked to Leofric around the year 1035, when as a couple they cultivated the friendship and spiritual guidance of Ælfic, prior of the Benedictine abbey in Evesham.[36] One can only speculate about her family background, though a forged charter claims that she was the sister of Thorold of Bucknall, sheriff of Lincolnshire, which was a relatively high position.[37] But since nothing is known about Thorold's family, the information only suggests that their parents were of some status. The location of Godgifu's largest estate in Newark, assessed at £50, along with another £25 of property in Nottinghamshire, suggests a family origin in that part of England. Given the impressive amount of wealth allotted to her in 1066, it can be conjectured that she came from a wealthy family, brought a considerable amount of land to her marriage, and perhaps acquired more through inheritance. Such a family origin would also help explain the logic behind her arranged marriage, because such unions among the aristocracy were often designed to forge bonds between powerful families from adjacent regions.

Though less wealthy than Leofric, Godgifu owned lands in eight counties assessed at over £160, and the village of Coventry was one of her possessions.[38] As a couple they collaborated to endow religious foundations. Some time before 1038 they provided for extensive restoration work at the Benedictine abbey of St. Mary in Evesham, the first of many such acts of generosity. Later, in a charter granting land to St. Mary's monastery in Worcester, their collaboration is signaled by a simple grammatical form, the Old English dual pronoun, which is used when they ask the monks there to intercede for *uncrum* souls and when they promise to be the guardians of the monastery's lands as long as *uncer* life lasts. In both instances the pronoun translates "of us both" and suggests an equivalence.[39] Another charter endowing land possessed by "Earl Leofric and Godgifu, the earl's wife" to Stow St. Mary's (near Lincoln) seems to be calculated to help the bishop of Dorchester, who had a large but modestly endowed diocese.[40] In addition they made joint gifts of varying amounts to convents in Much Wenlock and Leominster, to two churches in Chester, to a Benedictine abbey in Burton-upon-Trent, and to the cathedral in Worcester.

Their joint endowment of a monastery at Coventry in 1043 has been called "an extravagantly expensive act of piety" not merely because of the land involved, but also because (according to John of Worcester) they "made it so rich in various ornaments that in no monastery in England might be found the abundance of gold, silver, gems and precious stones that was at that time in its possession."[41] Many years earlier Coventry was the site of a convent. According to legend its abbess, St. Osburg, was martyred when it was ransacked in 1016. It lay in ruins until Godgifu and Leofric turned their attention to it and built a monastery on the site. In October of 1043 Eadsige, the archbishop of Canterbury, dedicated it to St. Mary, St. Osburg, and All Saints, and twenty-four monks under the leadership of Abbot Leofwine were established there.[42] In addition to endowing the monastery with extensive lands, Godgifu and Leofric built a shrine for St. Osburg which included a gold and copper reliquary enclosing her head. They also donated a silver reliquary containing the arm of St. Augustine of Hippo, which Æthelnoth brought back from Rome, where he had gone in 1022 to receive the pallium as the new archbishop of Canterbury. It is likely that Emma and Cnut, who collected relics as part of a larger policy of benefactions to the Church, acquired the relic from Æthelnoth, and it remained in the royal treasury until 1043, when the newly crowned King Edward wrested the treasury away from his mother Emma. Earl Leofric, who with other earls accompanied Edward, could have acquired it then and turned it over to the new foundation in Coventry.[43] In addition to other treasures, William of Malmesbury mentions that as she was dying Godgifu placed a string of gems used for prayer around the neck of a statue of Mary. Orderic Vitalis writes that Godgifu "lavished all her treasure upon the church: sending for goldsmiths she gave them her whole store of gold and silver to work into covers for gospel books, crosses, images of the saints, and other marvellously wrought ecclesiastical ornaments."[44] One of the artists they employed was a monk named Mannig, who had earned a reputation as a scholar, singer, scribe, illuminator, and goldworker before becoming the abbot of Evesham in 1044.

A later but revealing indication of Coventry's wealth concerns the manipulations of Robert de Limesey, a notoriously greedy bishop of Chester. He moved his episcopal see to Coventry at some point between 1095 and 1102 and received royal permission to become titular abbot of the monastery, which he proceeded to despoil of its portable wealth. According to William of Malmesbury, who wrote shortly after Robert de Limesey's death, he went so far as to scrape 500 marks of silver from the beam supporting the shrine that housed the reliquary of St. Osburg.[45] A more precise accounting of the monastery's wealth emerges from the

Domesday Book, where despite its relatively recent foundation St. Mary's in Coventry received a larger annual income than all but seventeen monasteries in England.[46] Yet the village adjacent to it, which was to become the bustling town of Coventry in later centuries, remained a small agricultural settlement.

As the wife of an earl, Godgifu was able to enjoy a lifestyle well beyond the level of most people in Anglo-Saxon society. Given the number of sources that mention her and Leofric acting in collaboration, it seems likely that they had a good working relationship as husband and wife. While little direct evidence survives, it is possible to combine bits from law, literature, history, and archaeology with some informed speculation to reconstruct what her day-to-day life might have been like.

By tradition, Godgifu's education as a girl would have emphasized textile handcrafts such as spinning, weaving, and needlework. As a line from an Old English maxim succinctly puts it, "A young woman's place is at her embroidery."[47] Because few textiles from this period have survived, we can only gauge the value and prevalence of such skills by other kinds of evidence, such as wills, which sometimes specify items such as clothing, wall hangings, bedclothes, and table-linen in the same way as jewelry. The famous Bayeux tapestry is the most complete surviving testament to the skillful needlework that would become known in later centuries as *opus anglicanum*. More accurately described as an embroidery, it was executed by Anglo-Saxon women at the direction of Bishop Odo of Bayeux shortly after the Norman Conquest. Objects associated with clothmaking would have had a practical purpose, of course, but they also assumed a symbolic indication of a woman's status in society. Archaeological excavation of early graves reveals that women were buried with elaborately ornamented implements such as thread boxes and spindle-whorls, which must have signaled something beyond their utility. An aristocratic woman, however, even one who prided herself on the skill of her own handiwork, would have servants to take care of much of the household's needs for cloth production. For her own clothes, a married woman like Godgifu would wear a long-sleeved floor-length gown, most likely embroidered at the hems and elsewhere. Her head would have been covered by a headband and a veil, pinned to her hair which was done up in a plait. Her undergarments would be linen, and instead of stockings a strip of cloth would be wound around her lower legs to her feet, which would be protected by flat-soled leather shoes. For warmth she would put on a hooded cloak fastened below the chin by a central brooch.[48] The cloak, like the gown, might be elaborately decorated with needlepoint and jewels.

In addition to clothmaking Godgifu would have learned a variety of household skills, but other dimensions to her education are more obscure. Of her ability to read and write we know nothing except that it seems she was able to sign her name to documents. Depending on her family's resources, more formal education was not out of the question, though in general literacy was the preserve of women and men in religious orders. Indeed some nuns in Anglo-Saxon England achieved a remarkable level of literary sophistication. Yet some lay women also could read and write. A tenth-century will by a woman named Wynflaed, for example, contains a clause near the end which bequeaths almost as an afterthought "everything which is unbequeathed, books and such small things," to a woman who has already been assigned other items.[49] The point is that books, which were expensive items throughout the Middle Ages, might nevertheless seem too trivial to single out in a will. Furthermore, what literacy consisted of in this period could range from the mere ability to sign one's name, to an ability to read (but not write) Old English, to a high level of competence in reading and writing Latin. For a laywoman of Godgifu's position, it is likely that her formal education was at the rudimentary end of the range. But because she would have clerks available to read to her and take dictation, she could afford the practical advantages of literacy without necessarily possessing the requisite skills herself.

Aside from the textile crafts, tradition also reserved two other areas to the oversight of women. Anglo-Saxon law codes assigned them responsibility for keeping household wealth secure in strongboxes or store rooms, to which they kept the keys. The seventh-century law code of Æthelberht, for example, states, "If a free woman in control of the keys does anything seriously dishonest [in that role], she is to pay thirty shillings compensation."[50] Though the precise meaning of the Old English term for the crime (*leswæs*) is ambiguous today, the hefty size of the fine indicates that it was considered a serious offense. The laws of Cnut specify that a woman could not be held responsible if her husband brought home stolen goods, as long as she did not lock them up. The implication is that a wife had personal control over certain household valuables independent of her husband, for which she assumed legal responsibility. Grave sites reveal that women (and not men) were often buried with keys or key-shaped objects, which symbolized how their role in managing the household economy formed part of their personal and social identity.

A third function associated with women was the welcoming of guests, which Old English literature describes in a highly conventionalized form. For example, after Beowulf arrives in Denmark and disposes of a verbal challenge by one of King Hrothgar's lieutenants, Queen Wealhtheow comes forward with a mead cup and offers it first to Hrothgar. She then offers it to each of the other retainers in turn until she comes to Beowulf, as if she considers him one of the lesser warriors because he is still young and unproven. The next day, however, after he has defeated Grendel, Wealhtheow repeats the ceremony during the celebratory feast. She gives the cup to Hrothgar with a reminder for him to be generous to Beowulf and his companions, then she turns to Beowulf, who now is sitting next to her two sons. She offers the cup to him, presents him with valuable jewelry and armor, and asks him to watch out for her sons, who (the poet implies) are in danger from their uncle. In so doing Wealhtheow uses her ceremonial function to transact some important dynastic business. While heroic literature like *Beowulf* does not imitate life in Anglo-Saxon England, other sources support the notion that wives of noblemen were expected to assume a prominent role in welcoming guests to a household, whether or not they offered a mead cup with as much eloquence or diplomacy as Wealhtheow.

For a number of years before Leofric's death in 1057 the couple's permanent home was located in Coventry, which was one of the estates in Godgifu's possession. Early chronicles give the impression that Leofric was often away from Coventry attending to public duties and advising the king. Most of the locations mentioned are south of Mercia, especially in the region around London and Canterbury, which is where the urgent affairs of the kingdom took place at this time. Godgifu accompanied him on at least some of these occasions, if a casual reference to her presence with Leofric and King Edward in Westminster Abbey is any indication. Even when official business of the kingdom subsided, each of them had estates scattered across Mercia and Wessex to visit. They also had occasion to call on the monasteries and other religious foundations that they supported in one way or another. In all, one gets the impression that Leofric and Godgifu did not lead a sedentary life in Coventry. Their affairs took them all over England.

The house they called home has not survived, mainly because it was built of timber, as were most structures before the Norman Conquest. It would have consisted of a complex of buildings, centered around a great hall for meals and for entertaining guests, the interior of which was painted various colors and finished with tapestried wall hangings. The

Beowulf-poet, for example, singles out how tapestries woven with gold thread added to the splendor of Heorot, and other literature describes how buildings used tapestries for decoration.[51] Contrary to the impression of drabness too often associated with the "Dark Ages," people of this time had a great fondness for brightness and color, which can be glimpsed today in the manuscript illuminations and jewelry that survive in pristine condition. Dyed wool and painted wood, however colorful to begin with, rarely survive the centuries. Whatever the precise details of Godgifu's material environment, it likely included expertly ornamented cloth and a range of vivid colors.

Her daily life would also include regular religious devotion, in which the monastery at Coventry presumably played a prominent role. The earliest reference to Godgifu and Leofric is in connection with their spiritual advisor of the time (Abbot Ælfic of Evesham, before they founded the Coventry monastery), and it was common for the household of an earl to enlist the services of a priest for secretarial and liturgical duties. Discussion of Godgifu's piety is more than speculative, because clerics took care to preserve records of their acquisitions in written documents.

Because so few firm details about her daily life survive, speculation about Godgifu such as that summarized above takes on a schematized and idealized quality: she worked with cloth, she traveled, she held property, her home had tapestries, etc. What are inevitably lost include her idiosyncrasies and quirks of personality: did she travel reluctantly? was she a vigorous manager of her estates? was her relationship with Leofric more turbulent than it seems? In Anglo-Saxon England, as in many societies up to the present day, women's rights were vulnerable to abuse, because whatever is proclaimed as custom and law can appear more optimistic than the lived reality for any comparatively defenseless group. For example, a husband with the right connections could use Anglo-Saxon law to repudiate his wife and take a new one, and little is known of the fate of those dismissed. A woman suffering abuse at the hands of her husband had little recourse unless her family was influential enough to intervene on her behalf. And aside from the role of wife or nun, a woman like Godgifu had no career options (unless one includes widowhood). Nevertheless, it would be disingenuous to assume trouble where no evidence for it exists, and Godgifu and Leofric give all the external signs of a good relationship. A final and perhaps telling indication is that they made explicit arrangements to be buried side by side in the abbey that they jointly founded in Coventry.

Leofric and Godgifu lived in Coventry for an unknown number of years, but long enough for the Old English *Vision of Leofric* to call it his "longstanding home." Coventry, along with the rest of Godgifu's lands, was forfeit to King William upon her death in 1067, if not the year before. She and Leofric had one child, Ælfgar, who succeeded his father as earl of Mercia in 1057. Ælfgar seems to have been as belligerent as Leofric was statesmanlike; he died before 1066. Two of Ælfgar's sons, Edwin and Morcar, also became earls. At one point they deprived their grandmother Godgifu of some of her lands, although it is not known what motivated their actions.[52] Ælfgar's daughter Edith (Ealdgyth) was a queen twice over: first to Gruffyd, king of North Wales until he was killed in battle against an English army led by two of Godwine's sons, Harold and Tosti, in 1063. Within a year Edith married the man responsible for making her a widow, Harold Godwineson. Harold and Edith's marriage briefly united the rival houses of the great earls of Wessex and Mercia. It even more briefly made Godgifu's granddaughter the queen of England when Harold succeeded Edward the Confessor. After Harold's death at the battle of Hastings, Edith was allowed to retire to the abbey of La Chaise-Dieu in the Auvergne, where for many years she was commemorated as an important benefactor.[53] As prominent as Godgifu was in the decades before the Norman Conquest, little else is known about her life. She died in 1067 and was buried next to Leofric in the abbey they founded in Coventry.

Although she was not one of the primary players in the grand political drama of her time, Godgifu had a close-up view, like an actor standing just upstage, on the rise and fall of the most powerful families in England. As an earl's wife she was a privileged woman who enjoyed a standard of living far above that of the vast majority of the population. But just as remarkable from our perspective are those things that mark her life as ordinary. From their home in the rural Midlands, Godgifu and Leofric apparently enjoyed a collaborative relationship throughout these turbulent decades, and until 1066 their family fortunes emerged unscathed from crisis after crisis. She was pious and generous in ways that were conventional for her day, and she controlled enough property independently to make her one of the wealthiest individuals in England. None of the earliest sources gives even a hint of what makes her famous today. That story was the product of a later generation.

Chapter 2

Godiva Emerges

For more than a century after Godiva's death, no written source makes even the faintest allusion to her legendary ride or to anything now commonly associated with it, such as nakedness, the horse, or taxation. For example, when Godiva's name appears in William of Malmesbury's *History of English Kings* (ca. 1126), she is eulogized as Leofric's saintly wife in a rather conventional way. Nothing would lead anyone to anticipate the sensational story that abruptly appears a century later, when chroniclers in the Benedictine abbey of St. Albans insert a fully developed narrative into their Latin histories. The story comes under the entry for 1057, the year of Leofric's death. After praising the couple's piety and their generosity to religious institutions, one account continues:

> Yet this pious countess, wishing to free Coventry from an oppressive and shameful servitude, often begged her husband the count, under the guidance of the Holy Trinity and the Holy Mother of God, to deliver the town from this servitude. And when the count rebuked her for uselessly persisting in demanding something ruinous to him, he firmly ordered her never again to raise this subject with him. She nevertheless persevered in her request and relentlessly exasperated her husband with it, until she finally forced this answer from him:
>
> "Mount your horse naked," he said, "and ride through the town's marketplace from one end to the other when all the people are gathered, and when you return you will get what you demand."
>
> And in response the countess said, "And if I am willing to do so, will you give me permission?"
>
> The count replied, "I will."
>
> Then the Countess Godiva, dear to God, mounted her horse naked on the day agreed upon and, by loosening the braids of hair on her head,

veiled her whole body except her brilliantly white legs. And when she had finished her journey unseen by anyone, she returned rejoicing to her husband, who considered it miraculous. And Count Leofric, releasing the city of Coventry from its servitude, confirmed its charter with the stamp of his own seal.

Once this narrative (quoted here from Matthew Paris's *Chronica Majora*, ca. 1250) was put into circulation, the earlier woman of pious reputation was eclipsed by the Godiva familiar to every subsequent century.[1] The anecdote is remarkable for containing so many elements that have become essential to the legend: Godiva's compassion for the citizens, her persistence as a nag, her audacity in agreeing to Leofric's terms, the ride itself, and her ability to complete it unseen by anyone. Just what the people's "servitude" consists of is not stated, though later manuscripts of the St. Albans chronicles identify it as a toll, a detail which may owe something to Matthew Paris's opposition to all forms of taxation. Whatever its origin, the toll or tax becomes a permanent part of the story. Aside from the miraculous elements, the mention of the toll is one of the first signs that the story is a fabrication, because it presupposes post-Conquest social and political institutions that would be anachronistic in Anglo-Saxon England (as discussed later in the chapter). But the tendency to project anachronisms has always been part of the legend's reception, because readers from every century approach it with preconceptions shaped by contemporary culture, and those preconceptions in turn shape the way the story is handed down to later generations. It may be impossible to read the St. Albans chronicles without imposing our own anachronisms, but the effort to consider it in its early context repays the trouble. How do the first versions, taken on their own terms, characterize Godiva?

They paint a surprising character portrait. Godiva is a clever and assertive wife, rather than the helpless victim of a cruel husband. Not only is her relentless (*indesinenter*) advocacy so exasperating (*exasperans*) to her husband that it forces (*extorsit*) a response from him, but other manuscripts make sure the point is not lost by rephrasing the sentence "She on the contrary, prompted by womanly obstinacy (*pertinacia*), persevered in her request . . .". She is more than a nag, however. There is an element of cunning in the successful manipulation of her husband, which finds parallels in other literature of the time. Her character resembles the "scheming wife," a stereotype in bawdy stories called fabliaux which were popular in France and the Low Countries during the decades when the Godiva legend first appears. This genre later became familiar to English-speaking audiences through Chaucer, who in the fourteenth century dusted off some old fabliaux for his *Canterbury Tales*, but even before Chaucer French versions circulated around England in manuscript form. In a typical fabliau, such as the one Chaucer used for the Shipman's Tale, a wife might use an outrageous stratagem in order to satisfy the lust of a local priest and to swindle money out of her merchant husband in the bargain. Typically the woman gets what she wants and escapes punishment. Although Godiva's motives are more virtuous than the adultery or greed of a fabliau wife, her persistence seems to be calculated with the same kind of cunning: if she pushes Leofric far enough, he might give a rash answer that she can capitalize on. He does just that. Rather than saying "no," he uses a rhetorical figure known as an *impossibilia*, which gives an answer that literally means "yes" but stipulates a condition that would be impossible or unthinkable to carry out (such as "over my dead body"). Though Leofric delivers his "ride naked through the town" response as an emphatic "no," Godiva turns it back on him and interprets it as a literal condition for releasing the citizens from their servitude. To clinch the point, when she explicitly requests permission to ride naked ("And if I am willing to do so, will you give me permission?"), she uses the prospect of humiliation to corner Leofric. In a way that is reminiscent of a fabliau husband, he is forced to choose between the shame of going back on his word by retracting the condition or the shame of sanctioning the public nakedness of his wife. Because he has legal rights over her body, her nakedness would be socially humiliating to him as well as to her. Yet once cornered, his best option is to grant permission in the hope that she will recoil at the thought of exposing herself. While the narrative emphasizes her compassion for the people, the promptness of her reply suggests that she has already decided on a plan. Concealing her body under her loosened hair allows her to fulfill the conditions while mitigating the humiliation. Just what "unseen by anyone" (*a nemine visa*) means in this story is not clear. If Godiva rode through the marketplace while it was filled with people, she could not have returned unnoticed. Taken literally the phrase implies that her hair was an effective substitute for clothes (even though her legs were exposed) so that most of her body was concealed. Like the "scheming wife" of a fabliau she gets what she wants and escapes unshamed.

The similarities with fabliaux suggest only that narrative elements for a woman using cleverness to outwit authority were generally available at the time that the legend first appeared. In keeping with Godiva's long-standing reputation for piety, however, her character fits almost as well in the genre of a saint's life as a fabliau. Like a saint she is motivated by selfless compassion for the citizens; she invokes the Trinity and the Virgin Mary; she is willing to abase herself for a higher good; and her ability to ride unseen by any of the citizens has a quality of the miraculous about it. The use of her loosened hair to cover her body may even have the biblical authority of a passage from 1 Corinthians: "if a woman nourish her hair, it is a glory to her; for her hair is given to her for a covering."[2] Leofric interprets her accomplishment *pro miraculo*, where the Latin phrase may simply mean that he finds her ruse astonishing, but it may also allude to divine intervention allowing her to ride through a crowd unseen. And like a saint she returns not smarting from the humiliation but rejoicing (*gaudens*) in her divinely appointed role. After all, Godiva the social activist is still as "dear to God" as she has always been.

But saintliness is not the first thing that springs to mind in the context of her ride because it clashes with the anecdote's worldly motives (tax relief) and not-so-subtle erotic details. The way that Godiva fulfills the condition of the ride is not left discreetly vague. The narrative takes pains to specify that she loosened her hair so that it veiled (*velavit*) all her body (*corpus suum totum*) except for her brilliantly white legs (*crura candidissima*). Godiva's hair and legs are, along with the horse, details that survive in nearly every version of the legend down to the present day. The hair as drapery that provides partial covering and the legs that escape concealment are well-attested fetishes which erotically charge Godiva's body in a way that simple nakedness would not. The most familiar example of such hair iconography throughout the Middle Ages is Mary Magdalene, who according to tradition was a prostitute before she changed her ways and dedicated the remainder of her life to penitence and solitary prayer as an anchorite. In some medieval illustrations her unbound and wild hair symbolizes the sexual promiscuity of her pre-conversion life, while in others the hair has grown until it covers her entire body and becomes a hair shirt of penitence which replaces her clothes.[3] Similarly, when the virgin martyr St. Agnes was stripped of her clothes and sent to a brothel, her hair miraculously grew "so long that it covered her better than any clothing."[4] To a medieval audience Godiva's state of undress would also call to mind Eve, whose naked body and unbound hair had contrary meanings: before the fall they were associated with innocence but

afterwards symbolized the sin and carnality of women and, by extension, the whole human race.

While such religious iconography is illustrative, it draws on social
codes that attribute a sexual value to women's hair. In medieval Europe it was the custom for a woman to wear her hair loose until marriage, after which she would not go out in public without putting it up
in a chignon. A married woman's hair would ordinarily be worn loose
only in private, only for her husband. For a married woman like Godiva
(even fully clothed) to show herself in the marketplace with loosened
hair would be seen as a public declaration of her sexual availability and
a scandal both to her and her husband. While unmarried women could
wear unbound hair without moral prejudice, its association with sexual
availability is graphically illustrated in the customary law of medieval
London, where prostitutes (who presumably wore their hair loose in
plying their trade) might be punished by having their hair cut short
before being paraded to the pillory "with minstrelsy."[5]

Godiva's position on horseback adds to the eroticism in the story,
because the horse has functioned as a symbol of sexual passion as far
back in Western culture as the Greek myth of Hippolytus, whose firm
control of his chariot horses is the physical equivalent of his stoic refusal to succumb to sexual temptation. In the end, after refusing the
advances of Phaedra, he is killed when the gods terrify his horses, who
stampede and drag him to his death. His fate is signaled in his name:
"Hippolytus" literally means "unbridled horse." A much-modified version of the Greek legend found its way into medieval England as the life
of St. Hippolytus, a third-century Roman bishop whose identity became confused with the older myth. He was martyred, the story goes,
by being torn asunder by horses. In Hertfordshire there was a church
dedicated to St. Hippolytus, where sick horses were led inside to be
cured at the saint's shrine.[6] The classical Greek myth was also known to
educated audiences throughout Europe. A twelfth-century satirist
known only as the Archpoet, for example, in writing of the temptations
of the flesh in a university town, complains (in John Addington
Symonds's translation): "If you brought Hippolitus / To Pavia Sunday, /
He'd not be Hippolitus / On the following Monday."[7] But the old myth
is not the only source of association between horses and lust. Even
today people speak of "unbridled" passions or giving them "free rein."
And the human posture of horseback riding, then as now, with the legs
straddling so much animal vigor, only adds to the association.

Both the horse and Godiva's hair are capable of eliciting a variety of interpretations, but one way to understand how they condition the reception of the story is to imagine how it would change if Godiva were said to have walked through Coventry, and walked without any attempt to conceal her nakedness. At the least it would inspire more pathos than eros. In Chaucer's Clerk's Tale, to cite a well-known story which both he and Petrarch borrowed from Boccaccio, Walter contrives to humiliate his wife Griselda by ordering her to walk from his palace back to her father's home dressed in nothing but her *smok* or undergarments.[8] While the overt moral of the tale is to underscore the virtues of submission to divine and human authority, the town's citizens (and the reader) primarily feel "pitee" and "rewthe" (compassion) for Griselda's nakedness. By contrast, the partial concealment provided by Godiva's hair and her position on a horse provoke quite a different response, even though her ride through the marketplace, like Griselda's walk, is done at the instigation of her husband and under the threat of public humiliation.

The narrative strategy of directing attention to Godiva's hair and legs puts the reader in the position of a voyeur, which is precisely the perspective denied to the town's citizens, if "unseen by anyone" is taken literally. The sense of transgression that is always a part of voyeurism serves to amplify the eroticism. By the twelfth century medieval authors had begun to develop sophisticated conventions that invited the reader to assume an intrusive perspective onto a private scene in a variety of literary genres including bawdy tales, mystery plays, chivalric romance, and religious lyrics.[9] In later centuries the Godiva legend occasioned the invention of Peeping Tom (discussed in chapter 4 below), which makes the theme of transgression explicit. But Peeping Tom merely formalizes the kind of readerly voyeurism that the legend has invited from its first appearance. Within the plot of the story the citizens of Coventry are forbidden to gaze, while readers are directed to imagine Godiva's exposed legs, her hair, and the whiteness of her skin. The narrative creates the imaginative conditions that forbid the gaze, then invites the reader to indulge.

Another element that contributes to the erotics of the narrative is the location of the ride within the marketplace of Coventry "when all the people are gathered." The context of buying and selling turns Godiva's naked body into a commodity that circulates among the other goods, yet she remains detached from the transactions. It is a precarious passage. Her returning unseen is the equivalent of her returning unpossessed: the one is as miraculous as the other.

From its earliest appearance in the thirteenth century, the story of Godiva's ride makes use of a number of culturally charged elements that account for its immediate appeal to other chroniclers and, later, poets. Moreover it places them in a socially respectable context that juxtaposes the high and the low. Is she a saint intervening for the good of the people with miraculous help from heaven, or is she a bawd offering a peepshow for money? Elements for both interpretations are present, as are other contraries: she is an aristocrat with empathy for the commoners; although manipulative she is obedient to her husband's authority; and although scandalously exposed she keeps her virtue intact. The enduring appeal of the story, however, is not in such compassion, compliance, or virtue. Rather it is in the way it fashions a woman's body as an erotic spectacle for the reader's voyeuristic gaze. How could such a remarkable story appear, as it were, out of the blue? The rest of the chapter takes up the immediate context of the St. Albans historians and speculates on the genesis of the story, including fertility myths; it then places the story in the context of Coventry's urban growth around the thirteenth century, and finally surveys the earliest retellings of Godiva's naked ride.

St. Albans

The earliest accounts of the naked ride (like that quoted at the beginning of this chapter) survive in several chronicles written by two of the most influential historians of medieval England, Roger of Wendover and Matthew Paris. At St. Albans they contributed to a robust tradition of history-writing in England which began shortly after the Norman Conquest, when scholars in ecclesiastical centers such as Canterbury, Worcester, Malmesbury, and Durham compiled comprehensive narrative histories for the first time in centuries, or more precisely, since the Venerable Bede (d. 735). The contrast in output before and after the Norman Conquest is striking: before 1066 the writing of synthetic histories among the Anglo-Saxons was almost moribund, yet by 1100 "more history was being written than ever before or often afterwards."[10] The variety and sophistication of the writing is at least as impressive as the sheer volume: "Everywhere there is order and method, intellect applied to the creation of books which are genuine works of reference and research."[11] John of Worcester (fl. 1130s) is typical of the twelfth-century historians who helped spread the laudable and pious reputation of Godiva and Leofric. He is especially noteworthy in this regard because he lived not long after the death of Godiva, and in an area (Worcester) where she and her husband would have been remembered as benefactors. An early version of John's chronicle found its way to Coventry and was probably copied there in the twelfth century. Although the Coventry manuscript includes an annotation to Earl Leofric as "the founder of this church" along with a few other references to him, no special notice is taken of Godiva.[12]

How to explain the sudden appearance of the narrative not in a skeletal form but fully elaborated with dialogue and a wealth of detail? It suggests either that the story of the ride had existed long enough to accumulate narrative elements in an undocumented history of oral transmission, which the chroniclers merely translated into Latin, or that it was a literary fiction fashioned by an author trained in Latin letters. If such an author worked with traditional sources, they are unlikely to be based on a deed performed by the historical Godiva, because nothing in surviving sources alludes to a naked ride through Coventry or to Godiva's role as an intercessor on behalf of the people. The main action of the story is inconsistent with the fact that Coventry was Godiva's possession. She did not need to make a desperate appeal to her husband. And if she ever did what the story attributes to her, it would be hard to explain how such a potentially scandalous deed escaped the notice of so many well-informed historians who mention Godiva and Leofric, such as Simeon of Durham (fl. 1108), Henry of Huntingdon (fl. 1129), John of Worcester (fl. 1130s), Ordericus Vitalis (fl. 1141), William of Malmesbury (d. 1143), Roger of Hovedon (fl. 1204), and Walter of Coventry (fl. 1217). Its absence would amount to a conspiracy of silence among twelfth-century historians.

The version quoted at the beginning of this chapter appears in the work of a later generation of historians, who lived some distance from Coventry, in St. Albans. Roger of Wendover (d. 1236) was the founder of the school, and his first and most distinguished successor was Matthew Paris (d. 1259).[13] Although Roger may have invented the story wholecloth, most of his writings were derived from pre-existing chronicles, and so it is likely some version found its way to him. It would not have been difficult. The Benedictine monastery of St. Albans was an important crossroads north-west of London and the first day's stopping point for nobles and clergy traveling to and from destinations in the north. It was used by laypeople and clergy alike, and at its peak it had a stable that could accommodate 300 horses. For the purposes of the

Godiva legend, it is interesting that in 1241 the prior and some monks from the Coventry monastery remained at St. Albans for a year, which is unusual only for the duration of their visit.[14] Because a variety of contacts between the two Benedictine houses were maintained, a story from Coventry, either oral or written, easily could have reached Roger of Wendover. Whatever its origin, once the story of the naked ride was put into circulation by Roger and Matthew, it quickly overwhelmed other biographical details about Godiva and Leofric. It was too compelling for later historians to pass up.

One source in particular, Matthew Paris's *Flores Historarium*, ensured the legend's wide availability because it "rapidly became one of the most popular history books of the age," surviving in numerous manuscript copies and serving as the basis for subsequent chronicles for centuries.[15] It remained an authoritative source even in the early modern period, after the arrival of printing. The first printed edition of Paris's *Flores* appeared in 1567 after undergoing tendentious revisions by Archbishop Matthew Parker to advance his reformist agenda, and he revised it again for a later edition in 1570. Though the liberties taken by Parker have been roundly criticized (for example: "Probably never has the text of any historical author been served so ill"), it must be remembered that factual accuracy was never the primary appeal of the *Flores*.[16] Matthew Paris "improved" sources such as Roger of Wendover's narrative by adding such stylistic touches as direct speech, similes, character sketches, and quotations from the Bible and classical poetry. To illustrate the lengths to which he might go, the following passage shows how Matthew transforms a simple list of names from Roger's *Flores* into a stinging denunciation.

> Fawkes, *lacking the bowels of compassion; the warlike and bloodthirsty* Savari de Mauléon with *his* Poitevins; William Brewer, *bellicose and experienced,* with his men; Walter Buc, *an assassin and man of blood,* with *his filthy ignoble Flemings and* Brabanters, *stained with every kind of crime . . .*[17]

The additions (in italics) have no known source other than Matthew's imagination, and they make Archbishop Parker's later revisions seem restrained in comparison. They also remind us that the writing of history was never viewed simply as a dispassionate account of empirical facts. As much as modern historians have praised Matthew Paris's prodigious output, lively prose, and diversity of sources, they have criticized him for having "literary airs and graces," for being careless, irascible, parochial, bigoted, and for writing like a journalist.[18] But these are the very qualities that make Matthew fascinating to read. They also make it easier to understand how the story of Godiva's ride might have appealed to him. It was no more and no less "historical" than other anecdotes in his chronicle.

Efforts to trace an origin beyond the St. Albans chronicles fall into two general categories, but neither succeeds in accounting for all the essential elements. Since the nineteenth century, folklorists have favored linking the legend with fertility cults that exclude men and involve a ceremonial action by a naked woman. Parallels with various folk customs can be found in India, central and northern Europe, Scandinavia, and Celtic Britain.[19] But the fact that "a naked female figure paraded before the people on horseback . . . seems to be hard to find" has not discouraged folklorists from finding the evidence worth attending to, because certain elements of Godiva's ride have a traditional quality to them.[20] The ancient Celtic Epona, for example, who as a fertility goddess and protector of horses appealed widely to Roman cavalry in first-century Gaul, appears seated (fully clothed) on a horse in early representations. The goddess Rhiannon, who first appears in *The Mabinogi* riding "a great, majestic pale-white horse, dressed in brilliant gold silk brocade," may very well be a later Welsh version of Epona.[21] Like Godiva, the goddess is a beautiful woman, who in riding her horse is not only an object of admiration but the cause of benefits to a community. Another folk tale found throughout Europe involves a young woman who solves a riddle-like test in which she must approach a king neither walking nor riding, neither clothed nor naked. She fulfills the conditions by straddling a goat and covering herself either with a net or her hair.[22] There is also a suggestive nursery rhyme, which reads, in an eighteenth-century version:

> Hight a cock horse to Banbury Cross,
> To see a fine lady upon a white horse,
> Rings on her fingers, and bells on her toes,
> She will have music wherever she goes.

Because the town of Banbury is directly south of Coventry, some folklorists have surmised that it refers to a local "Godiva-goddess ceremony" that lies behind both the legend and nursery rhyme. But no one knows quite what to make of it.[23] There is no textual evidence that it is as old as the Godiva legend. The rhymes, for example, would not work in

English before about 1600. But even if it proved to be ancient, to move from "Banbury Cross," Epona/Rhiannon, or any other fertility goddess to the legend of Godiva one must reconstruct the stages in an order such as the following: a pagan cult maintained an underground existence among the people of Warwickshire for centuries after their conversion to Christianity. Some time in the twelfth century the people transferred their veneration from the fertility goddess to Godiva at the urging of local monks who wanted to Christianize the cult. The monks then transformed the oral pagan myth into the written narrative which found its way to Roger and Matthew in the thirteenth century.[24]

Given in such stark terms, the hypothetical steps involved in such a reconstruction seem highly improbable. The only connection to the pagan rite would be the woman's position on a horse or, according to other legends, her nakedness. Even if such a fertility cult persisted, it explains little about the legend in its earliest narrative form. It has nothing to say about Godiva's motivation, the servitude of the people, Leofric's role, or the marketplace. Moreover, no surviving version of Godiva's ride makes a connection between the action that she performs and fertility. But even if one accepts such an origin, it skips over the most extraordinary stage in the process, which is the intervention of the monks, not the existence of a cult. It assumes that they convinced the people to Christianize the cult, as if Benedictines around the time of Robert de Limesey or the anarchy of King Stephen did such things. It then makes an additional assumption that they invented a narrative that thoroughly transformed the cult's paganism until it had little to do with fertility and far more to do with taxation and attached it to an Anglo-Saxon noblewoman otherwise famous for her piety. In short, as attractive as it may first seem, the fertility goddess hypothesis still leaves too much unexplained to be useful.

A second possible explanation depends on a literal misreading within another sequence of hypothetical events. It presupposes the existence of an earlier Latin narrative in which Godiva, in an appeal to her husband, is described as having stripped herself – figuratively – of all marks of rank (i.e., exchanging luxurious clothing for something simple). At some point an early chronicler misinterpreted a Latin word such as *denudata* as a literal rather than figurative description and, on the basis of this error, refashioned the story to account for Godiva stripped of all clothing and (by the same logic) with her hair loosened.[25] While this hypothesis has the advantage of plausibility in the semantic misreading of *denudata* and in the way it accounts for Godiva's supplication, it still explains only a fraction of the details of the legend in its earliest form. Like the fertility goddess theory, this one quietly passes over the most unusual stage in the hypothesis, which is the creation of a detailed narrative. It offers no explanation for the ride on horseback, the condition imposed by Leofric, the ruse of Godiva's hair as a covering, or the location of the ride in the town's marketplace. It also offers no corroborating evidence.

At heart, the *denudata* theory presupposes that the legend is based on a deed performed by the historical Godiva, written down at some point, and garbled in transmission. It also accepts the likelihood that Godiva humbled herself before her husband to obtain a favor for the townspeople. The historical Leofric, as earl of Mercia, wielded extensive power in the eleventh century, which no doubt made him subject to petitions of various kinds, but contrary to a basic assumption of this theory, he would not be in a position to release the people of Coventry from "servitude" or from a toll.

That privilege was Godiva's alone, because she – not her husband – held the land of Coventry directly from the king. Before any theory that seeks a historical origin for the legend can be believed, it must explain why Godiva had to humble herself to obtain something she already had in her power. The collection of a "tax" or "toll" from the "citizens" of Coventry is anachronistic on several levels. Because the peasants of Coventry belonged to Godiva's land or paid rent to her, she alone had the authority to release them from "servitude" or to determine how much to assess them. In the twelfth and thirteenth centuries an earl had the right to impose "tallage" on the people in his demesne, but the situation was different in Godiva and Leofric's lifetime.[26] One might hypothesize that the story's "toll" refers to a national tax, such as the infamous heregeld, which was a payment to support the king's soldiers and sailors, instituted in 1012 and continued until 1051. Like the ordinary geld, the heregeld was based on an assessment of land known as hidage, and some shires were assessed at a lower rate as a result of special intervention.[27] But the tax-collecting machinery was national, and if Godiva wanted a lower geld assessment it is likely she would have appealed to the king or his financial officers, not Leofric. An episode from Godiva's lifetime illustrates the way that the heregeld was collected. Shortly after Harthacnut was crowned king, he ordered Leofric and several other earls to join him in laying waste Worcester in 1041 (as discussed in the previous chapter). For five days they ravaged the town while the citizens defended themselves on Bevere Island in the

River Severn. The town's crime was that it not only refused to pay the heregeld but killed two of the king's officers sent to collect it. The political message was as unambiguous as it was brutal: the punishment visited on Worcester was national, not local. Otherwise Harthacnut would not have made a point of ordering earls from several parts of England to ravage the town. For the same reason the heregeld is unlikely to be the tax of the legend.

The persistent characterization of Godiva as lacking the rights of ownership and without the authority to act on her own is more consistent with post-Conquest social and political institutions than with late Anglo-Saxon England, where a woman like Godiva could hold a town like Coventry directly from the king, independent of her husband. Another detail points to a later origin: eleventh-century Coventry was scarcely large enough for the kind of market that the legend implies. Although it was destined to have a population of about 5,000 by 1280 and to become one of the largest urban centers in England by the close of the Middle Ages, Godiva's Coventry was a modest farming village that grew up adjacent to the monastery. The Domesday Book (King William's national inventory, completed in 1087), gives a detailed accounting of Coventry's population in 1066 and 1086. After listing several other landholdings belonging to Godiva, which became forfeit to William immediately after he assumed power, it reads (in translation):

> The same countess [Godiva] held Coventry. There are 5 hides. There is land for 20 ploughs. In the demesne are 3 ploughs and 7 serfs; and (there are) 50 villeins and 12 bordars with 20 ploughs. . . . [In 1066] it was worth 12 pounds. Now 11 pounds of weighed money.[28]

The five hides of land would cover an area of about 1,000 acres, and a "plough," which included a team of eight oxen, was an indication of how extensively the land was used for farming. The villeins, bordars, and serfs were different classes of peasantry (in descending order), the tallying of whom included only adult males, so the population was larger than the total of sixty-nine given in the passage. But even if the standard multiple is applied and the legend is superimposed on the demographics, it translates to an image of Godiva riding naked before about 350 of her own peasants in a small rural settlement next to the monastery that she founded with her husband. It is hardly the stuff of legend, and the legend can scarcely be historical.

The Growth of Coventry

In the absence of any other explanation, it is best to assume that at some point between 1067 and about 1200 someone, for unknown reasons, created the fiction of Godiva's ride in the form made familiar by the St. Albans chronicles. Other theories that have been proposed raise more questions than they answer, and each assumes, at a crucial stage that lies at the heart of the matter, that someone used pre-existing sources to fashion the narrative in all its essential details. If the story cannot be traced back to a historical event or to folk culture, what can twelfth- or thirteenth-century Coventry reveal about the way the legend might have arisen? Did it have local appeal? Did Godiva's ride, for example, serve as propaganda by allegorizing a conflict between the townspeople (Godiva) and heavy taxation imposed by the earl or some other authority (Leofric)?

The twelfth and thirteenth centuries coincided with a period of intense growth and economic development, not only in Warwickshire but all across England. The first "great inflation" in English history (ca. 1180–ca. 1220) brought about changes in the way that land was used. It was a period of legal reforms and of rebellions against the Crown, including the barons' revolt that led to the signing of the Magna Carta of 1215. The locality of Coventry was placed under the control of the earls of Chester by the twelfth century, and the town was selected as the base of power by "the ferocious and volatile" Ranulph II, whose rule from 1129 to 1153 (during the anarchy of King Stephen) was characterized by warfare against neighboring earls.[29] After 1145, however, his position weakened; he was arrested in 1146, surrendered his castles, and had to abide by a non-aggression pact from 1149 until his death in 1153. On his deathbed he restored to Prior Lawrence and the monks of Coventry the chapel of St. Michael, and granted a number of other chapels. His warlike ways did not keep him from policies that benefited the economic growth of Coventry, however. Merchants were encouraged to settle, for example, and those who built in the town were to be free of dues for the first two years. A charter from Ranulph II confirms the townspeople in their "burgage tenure," or the rent they were to pay the earl for their land and buildings. The same charter was confirmed by King Henry II in 1182 during a vulnerable period for Coventry in the minority of Earl Ranulph III (1181–1232), when Henry had appointed a custodian to oversee the town. When Ranulph III came of age he continued his grandfather's beneficial economic policies toward Coventry, even though he rarely visited the town. In 1218 he instituted a fair to begin on Trinity Sunday, and Coventry continued to grow in population and wealth. Throughout this period there seems to be no sign of friction between the earls of Chester and the burgesses of Coventry: no evidence of oppressive servitude or taxation which might give the Godiva legend an allegorical application. Just the opposite.

The abbey had its own interest in the town. Near the end of Ranulph II's reign a series of legal charters was forged to support the abbey's claim to half of Coventry and other outlying properties. It also secured certain judicial privileges and exemptions from a number of obligations, including "the payment of all dues to the king, to the king's reeve, to the bishop or to any man."[30] The charters were produced at a time when Ranulph was in a politically weakened state and during the anarchy of King Stephen's reign (1135–54), so that the chances they would be received as genuine were that much greater. Such forgeries, which were common throughout the Middle Ages, were not always written with a dishonest purpose in mind. They could be made as much in the interests of confirming liberties granted long before as in creating spurious ones. The Coventry forgeries were designed to help the monks to secure independence, or "liberties," from the authority of the local bishop, with whom they had had a tumultuous relationship over the years. The charters mark the beginning of the curious administrative division of Coventry between the earl's half and the prior's half.[31]

Coventry was not incorporated as a town (with its own elected mayor and other mechanisms of self-regulation) until 1345. While the twelfth and thirteenth centuries were a period of population and economic growth, they were also characterized by episodes of rebellion and war, economic inflation, and an administrative division within the town between the abbey and the earl. Against this background of growth and danger – what might be called the town's adolescence – the efforts of the inhabitants of Coventry to fashion a means of self-definition become easier to understand.

The forgery of legal documents and the creation of a fiction like Godiva's ride may seem to have little in common at first glance, yet they are both literary efforts to provide Coventry with a self-identity. The story of Godiva's ride need not have been produced in response to a political crisis or to advance one party's agenda. To free the town from an oppressive and shameful servitude (*a gravi servitute ac turpi liberare*), which is the earliest motive for Godiva's ride, is rhetorically analogous to granting liberties to a town beginning to develop a sense of autonomy. The story ends with Leofric granting a charter signed with his own seal. Aside from specific details, the St. Albans story leaves the impression of Coventry as a substantial urban center (*civitas*) united in its opposition to the earl, with a fascinating benefactress as its patron saint. It is, in an unconventional way, a myth of origin.

Such speculation cannot be pushed far, but a rival version of the legend can be located in Coventry in the years immediately preceding the chronicles of Roger of Wendover and Matthew Paris. It seems to point to an earlier, local provenance. Although now lost, it formed part of a Coventry chronicle attributed to Geoffrey, prior of the monastery from 1216 to 1235. Geoffrey's chronicle is no longer extant, but excerpts were paraphrased by Richard Grafton in the mid-sixteenth century and cited by William Dugdale in the mid-seventeenth century. Both Grafton and Dugdale were Warwickshire antiquarians who apparently were able to consult a local manuscript before it disappeared. When Geoffrey became prior in 1216 he was faced with the task of re-establishing the privileges confirmed by the earlier forged charters, many of which were seized and destroyed by Hugh, bishop of Chester, when he ransacked the priory in 1189.[32] His interest in both the legend and the forgeries suggests that each had a role to play in his understanding of Coventry and Coventry's understanding of itself.

Prior Geoffrey's chronicle, unlike those from St. Albans, has had no detectable influence on other medieval historians, and it may never have been copied for circulation outside Coventry. Because Dugdale merely alludes to it, Grafton's 1569 paraphrase is the only indication of Geoffrey's version of Godiva's ride.[33] It is significantly different from the narrative that emerged from St. Albans. It falls into two sections and begins with a (by now) conventional summary of the legend. Then he introduces the new material: "But Gaufride [Geoffrey] sayth that this gentle and good Lady . . . called in secret maner . . . all those that then were Magistrates and rulers of the sayde Citie of Couentrie," and explained the condition of the ride imposed by Leofric, which she "was well contented to doe." However, "for the reuerence of womanhed" she would do so only on the condition that

> streight commaundement should be geuen throughout all the City, that euerie person should shut in their houses and Wyndowes, and none so hardy to looke out into the streetes, nor remayne in the stretes, vpon a great paine, so that when the tyme came of her out ryding none sawe

her, but her husbande and such as were present with him, and she and
her Gentlewoman to wayte vpon her galoped thorough the Towne, where
the people might here the treading of their Horsse, but they saw her not.

When she returns after the ride with "her honestie saued, her purpose
obteyned, her wisedome much commended," her success left "her husbands imagination vtterly disapointed." The reader is not told why
Leofric's imagination was "vtterly disapointed," but this more likely concerns his expectation that she would not carry it through and deprive
him of tax revenues than a sexual fantasy involving his wife's public
nakedness (at this time an anachronistically modern interpretation).
Finally, after "shee had arayed and apparelled her selfe in most comely
and seemely maner, then she shewed her selfe openly to the people of
the Citie of Couentrie, to the great ioy and maruellous reioysing of all
the Citizens and the inhabitants of the same, who by her had receyued
so great a benefite."

It is almost certain that Grafton's is not a strict translation, although it
is impossible to know how much it departs from Geoffrey. His description of Coventry as a "City" with magistrates and other officials and the
incidental details of windows and streets are more consistent with an
urban setting closer to Grafton's century rather than late Anglo-Saxon
England or Prior Geoffrey. But even allowing for some embellishments,
the general features are clearly different from the version circulated by
the St. Albans chroniclers. The "streight commaundement" forbidding
the citizens from looking, which is new to Grafton, receives more attention than Godiva's physical appearance. Because it does not mention her hair, loosened or not, the reader may infer that she "galoped
thorough the Towne" without any attempt to conceal herself. Nor does
it specify her legs or any other part of her body. (Grafton may have
omitted some details because he was giving a second version of the
same story.) The narrative instead dwells on the details of the "out
ryding" itself to develop a sense of suspense whether the "streight
commaundement" would be effective in keeping the citizens from looking. The fact that her body was seen by a few people (husband, guards,
and servant) does not seem to lessen the accomplishment or compromise her modesty. Only after the ride when she is fully clothed are the
citizens allowed to gaze on her.

Another important difference is the relation between Leofric and
Godiva. Grafton presents the ride as a straightforward condition imposed by her husband, unlike the St. Albans chronicles, which make it

the unintended consequence of a rhetorical figure taken literally. He is not manipulated into allowing her to do something against his better judgment. She rides "for the freeing of the said Citie and satisfying of her husbands pleasure." While it would be wrong to take "pleasure" too literally in this context (as if her humiliation was nothing to him but a source of delight), this simple change introduces an element of cruelty into the character of Leofric. The St. Albans Leofric agrees to her request against his better judgment and later rejoices at the way Godiva miraculously avoids being seen or shamed. Grafton's Leofric finds the prospect of her public nakedness a source of satisfaction.

By 1569 when Grafton compiled his chronicle, the characterization of Leofric as villainous had evolved into a commonplace, so it is difficult to know how much of his phrasing is attributable to Geoffrey and how much to his own sixteenth-century preconceptions. But whatever the exact features of the story in Geoffrey's lost chronicle, its broader differences from the St. Albans version suggest that the story did not originate with either chronicler (that is, Roger of Wendover did not get it from Geoffrey, and vice versa). It is most likely that a version existed before 1216, though how much earlier and with what details is impossible to say.

Other Early Versions

A number of other early accounts of Godiva's ride circulated between Roger of Wendover and Grafton's 1569 chronicle. Grafton was a printer by trade, and in 1543, more than two decades before he published the version above, he published two separate editions of an obscure verse chronicle composed by John Hardyng, written about 1465. Each of the two printings of Hardyng's chronicle differs considerably from the other, suggesting that Grafton turned to a different manuscript source for each. Shortly after mentioning Matthew Paris's *Flores Historiarum* as a source for his knowledge of Coventry abbey, Hardyng summarizes the ride in two stanzas.

> Whiche Loefrike had a wyfe y^t Godiue hight,
> That naked rode throughout all Couentree,
> The tolles sore and seruage agayn right
> To redeme hole ayenste femynitee,
> She in her heare hangyng unto her knee,
> Vpon a daye, rode so through all the towne,

> To bye it free by her redempcion:
> For otherwise th'erle would not it free,
> But yf that she rode naked through the towne
> Vpon the daye that all men might her see,
> Trustyng she would not for no waryson
> Haue doen it so, by such redempcion;
> But thus by witte she kept her selfe vnshamed,
> And freed the towne, worthy was he blamed.[34]

It helps to have a prior knowledge of the legend to unravel Hardyng's labored syntax. The details of tolls and "seruage," of riding with her hair loosened, and using her "witte" to keep herself unshamed indicate Hardyng's debt to a version descended from the St. Albans chronicles. But it differs in making the ride a condition imposed by Leofric, which subjects him to the narrator's blame in the final line. While the marketplace is not mentioned, Godiva's ride is repeatedly characterized by images of buying. Besides the obvious "to bye it free," the repeated use of "redeme" and "redempcion" call attention as much to their etymological meaning of "to buy back" as a characterization of Godiva's act of salvation. The line "To redeme hole ayenste femynitee," meaning "to buy back in its entirety in exchange for her femininity," explicitly puts a market value on her sexuality, as if it could be used as an item of exchange. Another line that evokes the marketplace describes Leofric's speculation about Godiva's values: "Trustyng she would not for no waryson / Haue doen it so." The primary meaning of *warison*, a word that had a brief career in English between 1300 and 1600, is "wealth," though the *OED* notes that the phrase "to give [a woman] in warison" means to give her in marriage, from which derives a secondary meaning: "a maiden's honour." Though even Hardyng's admirers deplore the ham-handedness of his versification, his use of "waryson" in this passage is an inspired choice. It neatly conveys Leofric's calculation that Godiva would not compromise her virtue for any reward. Hardyng's two stanzas taken as a whole, though, do not elaborate the legend in all its details and make best sense as a summary of a story he could expect his fifteenth-century readers to know already.

While Hardyng takes the laurel for the first poetic version of the legend, his was not the first to adapt it from Roger of Wendover and Matthew Paris. In the fourteenth century John of Tynemouth, another St. Albans historian, repeats the story, as does John of Brompton.[35] The *Polychronicon* of Ralph Higden, a universal history down to 1342, whose popularity is attested by over 100 surviving manuscripts, was another vehicle that ensured the legend's dissemination. Higden was a monk who may have taken a special interest in the story because his monastery of St. Werburg in Chester benefited from Leofric and Godiva's generosity two centuries earlier. The *Polychronicon* was used as the basis for Henry Knighton's chronicle (in the 1360s), was translated into English by John Trevisa in 1387, and translated again, anonymously, in the fifteenth century. Trevisa's chronicle was printed by William Caxton in 1482, by Wynkyn de Worde in 1495, and by Peter Treveris in 1527. The *Polychronicon* summarizes the legend under the entry for the year of Leofric's death, 1057, which begins by itemizing the generous benefactions he made under the influence of his wife, and goes on (in the anonymous fifteenth-century translation):

> And at the instance of his wife he made the cite of Coventre fre from tolle, except the toll of horses; and to make the cite free from that tolle, the cowntesse Godgiva, his wife, did ryde naked thro the middes of the cite in a morowe, coverede but with here awne here.[36]

This abbreviated version preserves Godiva's insistence that Leofric free the town from tolls, the naked ride as a condition for lifting them, and her hair covering her body. However, it differs from earlier versions in associating the toll with horses, which has the effect of cheapening Godiva's self-sacrifice. A countess humiliating herself to alleviate a horse tax is more a plot for comedy than an inspiring exemplum.

From its first appearance the story of Godiva's ride has fascinated its audience, yet the story's early reception has its own interesting history. It emerged sometime before 1220 as a fiction posing as historical fact and linked to an eleventh-century Anglo-Saxon aristocrat who was otherwise famous for her generosity to religious institutions. The early St. Albans accounts present her as a rhetorically crafty woman who cajoles her husband into an improbable bargain for liberating the townspeople from an unspecified servitude or taxation. Her audacity in undertaking the ride is matched by her cleverness in averting shame. Popularized by the St. Albans chroniclers and propelled by its erotic theme, the legend spread until it was familiar in every part of England. By 1500 crucial details of the story had shifted, however, so that Godiva no longer maneuvers Leofric into an agreement he never wanted. He manipulates her, and as his character grows crueler she grows more helpless. Aside from Geoffrey of Coventry's lost chronicle, which had limited influence, the story circulated in two strands: a detailed version from the St. Albans chroniclers and an abbreviated version from Ralph Higden. No matter how the details vary, Godiva on a horse with her hair partially concealing her nakedness remains a provocative erotic image. While every version emphasizes her noble motivations and while it never descends to the obscene, the legend's overwhelming appeal can be traced to the perennial fascination of voyeurism. It did not matter that the story was fictitious, because historical veracity has never interfered with Godiva's popularity. After 1600 that popularity was exploited in ways that would have astonished Roger of Wendover and Matthew Paris, when Godiva's ride inspired provocative performances on the streets of Coventry.

Chapter 3

Godiva's Progress

Godiva's legendary ride lends itself to re-enactments because it is so simple – an individual riding a horse through the streets of a town – and because costuming tricks from the stage can rescue it from the scandal of public nakedness. The defining actions of most other famous individuals from England's past are harder to duplicate. Saints, for example, are commemorated for martyrdom or miracles; legendary heroes such as Guy of Warwick, Robin Hood and King Arthur are known for outsized deeds; even individuals from history strain the human capacity for mimesis, as Shakespeare and other Elizabethan dramatists remind us. But Godiva is different, and the city of Coventry recognized the potential of re-enacting her ride when in 1678 it included a Lady Godiva in the mayor's procession inaugurating the annual Great Show Fair. The introduction of Lady Godiva was a success from the start, as the pages below show, and drew large crowds from surrounding communities which the Coventry shopkeepers and tradesmen were happy to accommodate.

But was the 1678 procession the first? According to an anecdote that circulated in the early nineteenth century, the answer is no. It tells how in earlier years some citizens put on parodic processions that paraded a naked woman on a horse to ridicule the Roman Catholic doctrine of the eucharist. The anecdote's origin is obscure and comes centuries after the event it describes, and indeed it has the ring of what today would be called an urban legend. But the skillful way it weaves together events linked by legend or history to the town also gives it the quality of an insider's account. One version reads:

> It is well known that, before the suppression of the monasteries, this city was famous for the pageants displayed here, particularly those performed . . . on Corpus Christi Day, being one of their ancient fairs, the subjects

being taken from scripture, and exhibited with all that pomp and splendour which usually accompanied the Roman Catholic religion; large theatres were built for the purpose on high wheels, and were drawn through the principal streets of the city for the advantage of spectators. From these plays, it is asserted, the present show [including the Godiva procession] originated, for when the Roman Catholic religion was prohibited, they were continued, with many alterations, as a mockery; a naked woman on horseback was introduced to ridicule the Sacred Host – immediately after her came a Merry Andrew, to divert the populace with profane jests; he was drawn in a kind of house upon wheels, and, from looking frequently out of the window, acquired the name of Peeping Tom.[1]

The story goes on to say that on one occasion, the man playing Peeping Tom dropped dead upon leaving the "house upon wheels." After such a dramatic display of what looked suspiciously like divine retribution, no one dared to play the part again, "hence Peeping Tom has ceased to be part of the procession." This story is given some credence by the fact that since the first town-sponsored procession in 1678, Peeping Tom has been represented by a wooden statue, not an impersonator. Moreover, the statue antedates the 1678 procession by at least twenty years, because in 1659 a visitor to Coventry was told that it represented someone who was "stricken dead" for gazing on Godiva.[2] If some citizens once staged a mock procession to ridicule what they considered the empty ceremonies and superstitions of medieval Catholicism, their precaution with Peeping Tom shows that they were not beyond superstitions of their own. To substitute a statue would be a way of hedging their bets: while the parody targets the validity of the older ceremony, just in case they were wrong the statue might act as a lightning rod to divert future displays of God's wrath. And if the statue was once a saint's image, then the choice might be motivated by a wish for talismanic protection.[3] To this way of thinking, a Catholic God would not exact vengeance on a sacred image; a Puritan God would not care.

Whether or not the mock procession ever took place, all of the elements of it would be familiar to the citizens of seventeenth-century Coventry: Godiva's ride, the mystery plays, and the Corpus Christi procession. If such a procession *did* take place, the most likely period would have been between 1642, when Coventry came into the control of the parliamentarians during the Civil War, and 1678, when the more respectable town-sponsored Godiva procession is first recorded. While earlier decades cannot be ruled out, it is less likely that the Church of England in the reigns of Elizabeth and James would have tolerated a public mockery of the eucharist, which was still a sacrament and part of the liturgy. For similar reasons it is more difficult to imagine it after the Restoration of Charles II than before, leaving the period from 1642 to 1660 as the most plausible interval.[4] Precisely when it took place and even whether it took place are finally not as significant as the simple observation that in the mid-seventeenth century, the Corpus Christi religious procession and drama would still be an abiding memory from the town's not-too-distant past.[5] The effectiveness of the parody – or the outrageousness of the blasphemy – would depend on a Coventrian's knowledge of how the three elements relate. The "house on wheels" calls to mind the pageant wagons used in the old mystery plays.[6] The procession itself is modeled on the liturgical procession of Corpus Christi, when the consecrated host was carried through the streets of the town for all to see. Given the Roman Catholic insistence on the physical presence of Christ under the species of bread, the similarities between the two spectacles are unmistakable. "Hoc est enim corpus meum" means one thing in the context of the feast of Corpus Christi, but "This is my body" takes on an entirely different meaning in a Godiva procession. Each ritual makes the physical presence of a body the focal point of a public spectacle. Each commemorates a moment of salvation: one eternal, the other fiscal.

Using the foregoing account of the mock procession as a starting point, this chapter examines the period from the late Middle Ages to the Renaissance as a turning point in the legend of Godiva, when she evolves from a local curiosity to a national hero. The first literary elaborations appear, in which her character and that of her husband Leofric become fixed in important ways. A voyeur eventually given the name Peeping Tom is added. It also discusses what might be called the rhetoric of processions and the different kinds of spectatorship that the Godiva procession invokes. It starts by examining the history of two of the three events parodied in the mock procession, the pageant wagon and the religious procession, because of the surprising role they had in shaping the reception of the Godiva legend from the seventeenth century on.

The feast of Corpus Christi was introduced to England in 1318, and within decades became a popular occasion for elaborate civic processions. By design, it made the eucharist a special focus of piety and emphasized the importance of publicly viewing the consecrated host as well as consuming it.[7] Corpus Christi was observed on the Thursday after Trinity Sunday, ending the sequence of religious feasts following Easter. It was an important occasion (not the only one) for the clergy to educate the laity on the doctrine of transubstantiation. Based on the philosophy of thirteenth-century scholasticism inspired by Aristotle, the doctrine reasoned that even though the outward appearances of the bread and wine remained the same, the underlying "substance" changed to the divine flesh and blood. By 1318 the scholastic explanation was the Church's orthodox position, and the feast of Corpus Christi was part of a widespread and largely successful effort to disseminate the doctrine to the faithful.

The processions in Coventry were popular occasions that grew to involve the entire town by 1348, when the Corpus Christi guild was formed. The clergy played a central role, of course, but lay religious guilds managed the organization and finances, and representatives of the trade guilds and town government, decked out in their finest ceremonial splendor, made up such a large part that the processions were as much a display of Coventry's wealth and prestige as of its piety. In a typical year, the procession would begin at dawn, filled out by delegations from at least two dozen trade guilds carrying banners and wearing ceremonial gear. Near the front was the focal point of the procession, a monstrance containing the consecrated host held up by a priest for all the spectators to see. The sponsor of this part of the procession was not the clergy (as might be expected) but two religious fraternities. The Corpus Christi guild provided torches, candles, a crucifix, a gold and silver canopy, and a gold monstrance shaped like the sun with a glass compartment in the center to display the consecrated host. Four members of the Trinity guild, the most exclusive lay organization in Coventry, supported the canopy over the monstrance, which was held by the guild's chaplain. Other citizens and clergy followed the monstrance with appropriate liturgical ceremony: candles, a crucifix, hymn-singing, and incense. Still others were costumed as the Virgin Mary wearing a silver gilt crown, the angel Gabriel holding a lily, the twelve apostles, St. Ursula's virgins, St. Margaret, and St. Catherine. Even Herod, a star attraction of the dramatic pageants shortly to follow, had a place.[8] They were followed by the mayor and other representatives of the town government. By incorporating mercantile, governmental, and religious elements, the Corpus Christi procession became a ritual projection of civic unity.[9] Nor was it the only such occasion. It was simply the most elaborate of dozens conducted during the year. "Processions were the city's delight, common entertainment, and visible emblem of civic distinction," in which every element of the community was symbolically defining itself before the gaze of the townspeople.[10]

The civic unity was stratified, however, and not the kind of democratic equivalence that "unity" might suggest today. The ostentatious display of the social hierarchy reinforced the oligarchy of Coventry's most powerful citizens, especially the members of the Trinity guild and Corpus Christi guild, from whose ranks the mayor was chosen.[11] The stratification could lead to antagonism between levels of an urban society that had its moments of civil unrest. In 1387, for example, the "commons" of Coventry rose and, in an act of theatrical protest, "they threw loaves att the Maior's head in Saint Mary Hall."[12] Yet at a basic level the symbolism of the processions reinforced a feeling of cohesiveness that they ceremonially displayed. Otherwise they would not have been so well attended and supported with so much civic energy for hundreds of years. Because of their public prestige, the trade guilds competed for places of precedence in them. In a town of up to 10,000 people in the centuries considered here, they involved the entire population either as spectators or participants, because every citizen was associated in some way with a guild. Translated into terms familiar to us today, guilds combined the functions of social clubs, religious organizations, local politics, neighborhood parties, re-enactments of local history, and theatrical entertainment.[13]

Despite the strong admixture of non-religious elements, the Corpus Christi processions were prime targets of reformist zeal after the 1530s because of the ceremonial nature of the religious worship at their core. Barnabe Googe's "Popish Kingdom" of 1570 satirizes both the extravagant production involved in the older procession and the theologically controversial doctrine behind it:

> Then doth ensue the solemne feast of Corpus Christi Day,
> Who then can shewe their wicked use, and fonde and foolish play?
> The hallowed bread, with worship great, in silver Pix they beare
> About the Church, or in the Citie passing here and theare.

Googe's witty satire does not specify a town, but it gives a number of details that can be located in Coventry, including a canopy of silk and gold held by four citizens to protect the pyx, the characters St. George, St. Catherine, "Faire Ursley, with her maydens all" and a pageant wagon for the devils. It continues:

> The straunger passing through the streete, upon his knees doe fall:
> And earnestly upon this bread, as on his God, doth call.
> For why, they counte it for their Lorde, and that he doth not take
> The forme of flesh, but nature now of breade that we do bake.[14]

Although the feast of Corpus Christi and the processions satirized in the poem had ceased over twenty years earlier, the "popish kingdom" was still a threat to Low Church reformers such as Googe, whose rhetoric maintains a clear distinction between "they" and "we." This antagonism was not a subtle theological abstraction but a radical reformulation that affected everything from religious observances to the social and even epistemological basis of Christianity.[15] Only the most radical reformers sought to reject the ceremonial in all walks of life, however. It is a commonplace that ritualized processions were a vital part of Elizabethan statecraft, for example, and that a cult of the Virgin Queen developed as a replacement for that of the Virgin Mary.[16] Whether or not the later Coventry processions were a "repudiation" of the earlier Corpus Christi processions, the Godiva substitution coincides with a general secularization of public ceremony in early modern England.

After Coventry's Corpus Christi procession wound its way to the cathedral at the center of town for a solemn mass, the citizens returned to the streets for another kind of procession: the dramatic pageants. Toward the end of the fourteenth century, Coventry began to stage what has become known as the Corpus Christi cycle, a series of plays derived from episodes of the Bible, staged by the trade guilds. Similar dramatic cycles were produced not only throughout England but throughout western Europe. They are sometimes known as "mystery" plays, the word referring not to a religious mystery but to the trade or occupation of the citizens who staged the plays (this sense of the word deriving from Latin *ministerium*, "occupation"). The texts of only two of the original ten Coventry plays survive: *The Pageant of the Shearmen and Taylors*, which covers the annunciation, the nativity, the adoration of the Kings, and the slaughter of the innocents; and *The Weavers' Pageant*, which covers the purification of Mary and the disputation in the Temple.[17] The purpose of these pageants was to compress into a single day a series of staged episodes recounting salvation history up to the Last Judgment. Other towns had a larger number of shorter plays. In York there were as many as fifty – so many that in any given year it was impossible to stage all of them in one day. As a didactic medium they taught or reinforced episodes from the Bible to a largely illiterate population. The Tudor jest book known as *A Hundred Merry Tales* gives the story of a Warwickshire curate who, though "no great clerk nor graduate of the university," preached to his congregation on matters of faith and added, in an appeal more rhetorical than intellectual, "if you believe not me then for a more sure and sufficient authority, go your way to Coventry and there ye shall see them all played in Corpus Christi play."[18] Readers then and now are amused at the naivety of the curate's invocation of this "sure and sufficient authority," but the larger point (and the reason the humor can work at all) is that the pageants were an effective means of reinforcing the doctrine of salvation history.

The anecdote of the mock procession implies that after the suppression of the monasteries (in 1538) all of the ceremonial action associated with Corpus Christi ended. But religious processions were not finally eliminated until 1547 under Edward VI (when the religious guilds that organized them were also dissolved), and the feast of Corpus Christi was abolished the following year, 1548. The Coventry pageants, on the other hand, continued until 1579, when they were finally "layd downe" in Elizabeth's reign because of their lingering Roman Catholic associations.[19]

In Coventry and elsewhere the pageants survived so long after their original raison d'être, the feast of Corpus Christi, had been removed, because of their appeal to the laypeople, not because they were comfortably orthodox under the new regime. Even before Henry VIII they were denounced by some, and as early as the late fourteenth and early fifteenth centuries a popular reform movement known as Lollardy anticipated many of the criticisms now associated with the Reformation. Lollards found the drama's amateurish portrayals of God and Christ an intolerable affront to what was most sacred and ineffable, but what they advocated did not become institutionalized until after the Reformation. In the early 1560s the Mary plays were eliminated from the York cycle, and others elsewhere were "perused, amended and corrected" to adjust to the new orthodoxy.[20] A stanza in the Towneley play of John the Baptist, for example, which refers to the "worthy sacrament" of baptism and six others, was crossed out in red ink, framed in black, with "corected & not playd" added in the margin.[21] But for the most part the townspeople were less concerned about theological controversies than the enjoyment of staging and watching their productions. In 1556 for example, during the reign of Catholic Mary, John Careles, a Coventry weaver, was imprisoned for his Protestant beliefs. Because "he was there in such credite with his keeper," he was temporarily released to perform his role in his craft's pageant, *The Purification of Mary* and *The Disputation in the Temple*. When it was over "he returned agayne into prison at his houre appointed." Two years later, after being transferred to a London prison, he was burned at the stake for his antipapist convictions.[22] His case illustrates how the mystery plays could be sustained by a long tradition that existed on the fringes of the theological controversies of the sixteenth century. Produced as a largely civic event by lay guilds, the pageants' relative separation from the ecclesiastical hierarchies helps to account for their longevity.

At the height of their popularity the pageants annually drew over 10,000 spectators into Coventry from as far away as London. Writing in 1656, William Dugdale reports, "I have been told by some old people, who in their younger years were eye-witnesses of these Pageants so acted, that the yearly confluence of people to see that shew was extraordinary great, and yeilded no small advantage to this City."[23] Dugdale attended grammar school in Coventry between 1615 and 1620 and had other personal ties to the town, so his secondhand report may be credible, since "some old people" could very well have seen the pageants forty years earlier, before they ended in 1579. Local lore even has it that as a boy William Shakespeare attended the Coventry pageants, and that when Hamlet tells a visiting actor how a performance "out-herods Herod," it alludes to Coventry's Herod, famous for his extravagant raging. Local historians like Dugdale have always taken pride in pointing out that members of the royal family witnessed plays on at least twelve occasions from Henry V (1416) to Elizabeth I (1566, 1567, 1575). Few of the recorded visits coincide with the feast of Corpus Christi, but the citizens were ready to put on elaborate processions that included some Corpus Christi plays, as they did in 1566, for example, when four were staged for Queen Elizabeth.[24]

Perhaps another measure of the vitality of the Corpus Christi procession and pageants is the fact that they persisted, despite the considerable trouble and expense they entailed, throughout the long decline suffered by Coventry from the 1450s, when the population was about 10,000, to the 1550s, when the population had shrunk by about half, to between 4,000 and 5,000. In this period the wool trade (the basis of Coventry's economic prosperity) became depressed, on top of which came a crippling combination of crop failure, epidemics, and heavy taxation.[25] Economic recovery did not begin until the 1570s and then progressed slowly. Yet in spite of its misfortunes, Coventry maintained its processions and pageants as long as the authorities allowed them. They did not fade away for lack of interest, and even after 1579, when the pageants were officially "layd down," the town continued to put on theologically correct drama such as *The Destruction of Jerusalem*.

The details of the late medieval Corpus Christi ceremonies are of more than incidental interest, because the collective memory for these civic events almost certainly lingered. Though the religious processions and pageants ended about thirty years apart (1547 and 1579), each was sustained with great energy by the citizens of the town for about 200 years, and, as we have seen, as late as 1656 William Dugdale recalled hearing about them from an earlier generation. One can imagine a parodic Godiva procession in the seventeenth century as belonging to a time when the older religious processions and pageants were still alive in the town's collective memory (as with William Dugdale), perhaps all the more a target of anti-papist mockery because of the presumed threat from Roman Catholicism for much of this time. The doctrine of the eucharist remained for many decades a lightning-rod for reformist zeal. The anecdote asserts that the more respectable civic processions, dating from 1678, took their origins from such mock processions. It also implies that more than one mock procession took place.[26] What is less speculative is that as early as the fifteenth century a civic procession did indeed take place on the Friday of Trinity Week, in which Coventry's mayor, attended by armed guards, minstrels, and members of the craft guilds, went about proclaiming the opening of the Coventry's Show Fair. The opportunity for religious mockery existed, but did it ever take place, especially with such dramatic and irreverent wit?

Whether it did or not is ultimately unimportant to the larger point, which is that the Godiva procession first recorded in 1678 and held annually thereafter contained at least the potential for religious parody. Even if one dismisses the anecdote as a fiction of Roman Catholic propaganda, the later procession was conspicuously similar to the medieval one. Part of the prestige, in fact, was its medieval antiquity. It was held on the Friday of Trinity Week, the day after Corpus Christi, a movable date that was reckoned by the ecclesiastical calendar. Representatives of the trade guilds, the mayor, and other civic leaders still marched, as did guards in armor and representative saints, though Gabriel, Mary, Ursula, and the apostles were replaced by St. George and Bishop Blaise (the patron saint of woolcombers). Given the structural similarities between the two, it does not take an explicit mockery of the host to see the most striking substitution: the body of a woman impersonating Godiva replaces the body of Christ.[27] The Christ/Godiva substitution has at least one seventeenth-century precedent. A stone cross with religious images engraved on it had stood in the center of town at Cross Cheaping since the early Middle Ages.[28] In a moment of iconoclastic enthusiasm the town council in 1609 ordered the statue of Christ to be removed from the cross and replaced with an image of a naked Godiva.[29]

Over the decades after 1678 the blasphemous edge of the secular procession softened or the parallels were dismissed as trivial. But if at first they were prominent, and if scruples about offending religious sensibilities existed, they were overwhelmed by the attractiveness of profits from tourism the procession brought. The Lady Godiva procession became tremendously popular, drawing tens of thousands of visitors, and was held annually until 1769, and at irregular intervals thereafter until recent years.[30] The mayor and other members of the town government formed part of the procession until 1829, which was the year of the Catholic Emancipation Act, the legislation which permitted Catholics to be elected to the Commons and Catholic peers to sit in the House of Lords. Even though the emancipation concerned national elections, it reflects broader social changes in the first half of the nineteenth century which made it imprudent for politicians to risk popular support because of an insult – intentional or not, historically accurate or not – to the religion of a substantial number of voters. In this regard it is worth noting that the earliest copy of the anecdote, which adopts a strongly partisan Roman Catholic perspective, dates from the decades immediately preceding the Catholic Emancipation Act.

The account conflates the Corpus Christi procession with the dramatic pageants. The two occurred on the same day in late medieval Coventry, but they were always distinct events. After the religious ceremonies were over, the pageant wagons were rolled through the streets to the appointed stations where the plays were to be staged. But the author's confusion is understandable, since the mock procession he describes mixes together elements of all three events. The last of the three to be considered is the legend of Godiva.

What was the popular reception of the legend from the late Middle Ages into the early modern period? Even without considering the numerous texts circulating the story, there is ample evidence that the citizens of late medieval Coventry knew it and affectionately identified their town with Godiva. By the sixteenth century she had acquired some of the trappings of a local saint: on the feast of "Dame Goodyves" day members of the Cappers' Craft were required to attend mass.[31] In 1656 Dugdale described a window in Trinity church, which he estimated to date from the time of Richard II, which showed the heads of Leofric and Godiva facing one another. In the background was painted a woman in a yellow dress, side-saddle on a horse, and below the couplet:

> I Luriche for love of thee
> Doe make Coventre Tol-fre

Only fragments of the window remain, but the sentiment of the couplet suggests that it refers to an older version of the legend, in which Leofric is not villainous.[32] About 100 years after the window was made, in 1495, Godiva's name was invoked in doggerel verse affixed to the north door of St. Michael's church protesting a new fee for apprentices imposed by the city government as well as other tolls on wool and cloth.[33] Part of it reads:

> Be it knowen & vnderstand
> This Cite shuld be free & nowe is bonde.
> Dame goode Eve made it free;
> & nowe the custome for woll & the draperie.[34]

The spelling of her name as "Dame goode Eve" is a suggestive piece of folk etymology linking Godiva and Eve. While one is famous for an act freeing people and the other for an act subjecting them to bondage, both are identified by their nakedness and the shame that comes with it. Both are founding mothers. Because Eve appeared with Adam as a character in the annual *Cappers' Pageant,* her costume would have associated her with nakedness just as readily as Godiva was.[35] All of the incidental references from Coventry presuppose a wide acquaintance with the legend of Godiva's ride.

The St. Albans chronicles, especially Matthew Paris's *Flores Historiarum,* were reprinted several times in the early modern period, as were other medieval chronicles containing the legend of Godiva's ride. It was also reproduced in a number of early modern histories, some of which have been discussed already: Robert Fabyan (1533), Grafton (1569), Holinshed (1580), Camden (1586) and his translator Holland (1610), and Dugdale (1656). Some of these give it in a much-abbreviated form, as if they could presume their readers would know the details. This list gives an idea of the spread of the legend and the form it assumed in the years leading up to the 1678 procession in Coventry's Great Show Fair.

Though John Hardyng was the first to put the legend into verse, Thomas Deloney seems to be the first to fashion a literary (as opposed to historical) account in his ballad "Coventry made free by Godina [*sic*] Countess of Chester." Deloney, who started as a Norwich silkweaver and who is better known today for his prose fiction, was a prolific ballad writer. By 1596 (perhaps earlier) his ballads were collected and published under the title *A Garland of Good Will,* which was reprinted a number of times in the seventeenth century.[36] "Coventry made free" was later published in the 1723 *Collection of Old Ballads* (with an engraving of Godiva by John Pine; plate 1), which in turn formed the basis for a London broadsheet around 1750, which also included the engraving.[37] But like other printed ballads from this time, Deloney's presumably enjoyed an oral circulation as well.

Composed in seventeen four-line stanzas, it begins with praise for Leofric for granting the town many privileges. But Leofric has one character flaw: he insists on maintaining a toll on horses. Godiva entreats, he resists; he asks:

> "but what wold you performe & doe,
>   to haue the matter done?"
> "why, any thing, my Lord," quoth shee,
>   "you will with reason craue."[38]

He imposes the condition in a crucial stanza:

> "if thou wilt stripp thy clothes off,
>   & heere wilt lay them downe,
> & att noone-daye on horsbacke ryde,
>   starke naked through the towne,
> they shalbe free for euermore."

She is "much abashet" at this "strange demand" but agrees. She sends magistrates through the town to urge the people, for love of her and her good will for them, to "keepe their houses, & shutt their dore, / & clap their windowes downe" so that no one should see her. The ballad ends:

> And when the day of ryding came,
>   no person did her see,
> sauing her lord. after which time
>   the towne was euer ffree.

The edict enforced by the town magistrates reveals Deloney's indebtedness to Grafton, but some details in the first half point to a version of the St. Albans account. The ballad's melodramatic tone and slapdash

Plate 1 John Pine, engraving of Lady Godiva, ca. 1723

pace make Leofric's villainy as well as Godiva's self-sacrificing virtue more stereotyped, even comical. It is difficult to read it as a legend with a serious moral message, and with a few adjustments it could be made into a farce. Deloney's Godiva is clever in obtaining what she wants, with a relatively light demand on the citizens, who simply need to remain indoors and avert their eyes.

Where Deloney's ballad appealed to popular tastes, Michael Drayton recast the legend for a more educated readership in his eulogistic chorographic poem of England, *Poly-Olbion*, published in 1613. Drayton admired Deloney's poetry, calling it "full of state and pleasing," and he could have known the Godiva ballad, though there is no obvious verbal parallel.[39] The *Poly-Olbion*'s central subject is the land of England – its rivers, hills, forests, and mountains – with only passing attention given to the land's inhabitants. The poem's length, its hexameter couplets, and its tedious progression from one region of England to another might have appealed to Drayton's peers, but it was not a popular success. A large portion of the passage on Coventry is given over to the Godiva legend.

> [Coventry,]
> By Leofrick her Lord yet in base bondage held,
> The people from her Marts by tollage who expeld:
> Whose Dutchesse, which desir'd this tribute to release,
> Their freedom often begg'd. The Duke, to make her cease,
> Told her that if shee would his losse so farre inforce,
> His will was, shee should ride starke nake't upon a horse
> By day light through the street: which certainly he thought,
> In her heroïck breast so deeply would have wrought,
> That in her former sute she would have left to deale.
> But that most princely Dame, as one devour'd with zeale,
> Went on, and by that meane the Cittie cleerly freed.[40]

Drayton, who grew up in Warwickshire, drew from a version derived from the St. Albans chronicles, but like other chroniclers of this period he made the ride a condition. Godiva's characterization combines wifely submission (she "begg'd" Leofric) with allusions to more assertive virtues: her "princely" nobility, her "heroïck breast," and her all-consuming "zeale." While Drayton's Leofric clearly expects her not to make the ride, the condition comes across as more of a heavy-handed imposition, an exercise of his will "to make her cease" her supplications. For her part there is no room for clever maneuvering, as with Deloney and the earliest St. Albans versions. There is even the implication that her public humiliation would somehow compensate him for the revenue that would be lost ("if shee would his losse so farre inforce"). Her motivation is equally irrational, if still heroic. The ride itself is only alluded to, as if Drayton could assume that his readers would be familiar with it.

In both Deloney and Drayton the erotic element is treated gingerly and reduced to what is, interestingly, the only phrase common to both: Godiva is "stark naked" on a horse. Unlike the earliest St. Albans chronicles, these two narratives do not direct the reader's imagination to her loosened hair and exposed legs. Instead more attention is given to characterizing Leofric's coerciveness and Godiva's victimization. He imposes the condition, she recoils at the thought, though she finally endures it for the sake of alleviating a burdensome tax.

As the last chapter pointed out, the intercession by public officials to keep the citizens from looking while Godiva rides through Coventry is new to Grafton, and it is picked up by Deloney. Both use it to show that while Godiva is motivated by love for the citizens, she does not trust them. They require the threat of a public proclamation to keep every door and window closed and to prohibit anyone from looking. Though the edict is not in Drayton's poem, it became more common in accounts of the legend after Grafton's chronicle and Deloney's ballad. The moment that public authorities intervene, however, one can anticipate a figure to emerge who defies the edict.

He first appears, appropriately enough, as an anonymous shadowy figure in the seventeenth century, but by 1800 he acquires the name Peeping Tom and the occupation of a tailor. In important ways Peeping Tom becomes a surrogate for the reader (or viewer) of the legend, both of whom are tempted to "gaze" on the woman's naked body, even though such gazing is forbidden. Yet like the "Merry Andrew" in the wagon quoted at the beginning of the chapter, only Peeping Tom is punished, which makes him a scapegoat for the illicit voyeurism that goes on in the reader's imagination or collectively in the crowd. The next chapter discusses the evolution of this new addition to the legend, which may not be a literary invention but a character derived from a performer's role in the early Godiva processions.

However they interpret processions, most scholarly studies assume that the meaning of such rituals depends on the rhetorical figure of metaphor. They say, for example, that the city is a procession in the same way that the city might be a hive of activity. But another rhetorical figure is even more applicable: metonymy, the substitution of a part for the whole (for example "the pen is mightier than the sword"), where the pen stands for "literature" not by metaphorical substitution, but by extension, since the pen is part of what is used to create literature. Likewise, "sword" rhetorically includes "war" by a similar extension. Each object constitutes an essential part of the referent to which its figurative use points. In this sense they are unlike metaphoric substitutions, such as the human body for political organization or a rose for a man's beloved, where the figure invoked has no physical connection with the signified. When a military state parades large numbers of its armed forces, the rhetorical force is generated by the common perception that the display is only a part of a larger whole. Everyone knows it is a metonymy, whether or not they can name the trope.

Processions such as that for Corpus Christi and for civic occasions create a unifying ritual by incorporating representatives from all parts of society as it was conceived at the time, which in medieval Coventry meant trade guilds, the town government, and the clergy. When the Bakers and Weavers marched, for example, their banners and emblems of the trade were less meaningful than the (metonymic) physical presence of a number of masters and journeymen walking in the procession. Even though the participants were exclusively male and weighted toward the well-to-do, they represented every craft member and thus, by extension, every member of the household (men, women, children) associated with the trade. And after 1536, when every householder was legally obligated to be affiliated with a trade guild, the procession's symbolism extended to include virtually every citizen of Coventry.[41] Similarly every member of the clergy, as well as every member of the town government was represented by metonymic extension. So in spite of the hierarchy they reinforced, the rhetoric at its most basic level gestures toward inclusivity and civic unity.

While in a town like Coventry there were many civic and religious processions throughout the year, at Corpus Christi the semiotics are especially loaded because of the theological doctrine it commemorated. Of course the eucharist has its conventionalized metaphors such as "the bread of life," but a compressed metonymy lies at the heart of the theology of transubstantiation, by which the part (the consecrated host) not only signifies the whole (Christ) by extension, but the part miraculously *becomes* the whole, and the whole is present in its entirety in each part. According to this doctrine each host, down to its smallest fragment, is part *and* whole at the same time. The theology of transubstantiation was not the exclusive province of a priestly caste of experts; it was preached widely to the laity starting when the feast of Corpus Christi was introduced in 1318. Over the years the populace developed more than a passing acquaintance of the dynamics of the part-for-the-whole extensions that were at the center of the doctrine of the eucharist, especially in light of the annual processions that brought God physically through the streets of their town and the frequent rituals on the altar. If one considers the Corpus Christi procession from the perspective of its dominant rhetorical device, metonymy, it is a short step to understanding the citizens' eagerness to appropriate it for other uses.[42] Of the many civic and religious processions in medieval England, none could equal Corpus Christi's rhetoric of unity, in which the part and the whole are miraculously inseparable.

As before, I want to bring the discussion back to the anecdote's mock procession. In light of the weighty rhetoric of the Corpus Christi procession, just what does it mean to substitute the body of a woman for the body of Christ? Once the religious parody has done its work, what other meanings remain? Of what "whole" is her body a part? Does she project a kind of unity? Or is her rhetoric a kind of anti-metonymy, not signifying anything beyond herself, a display of the body as its own signification: a rhetorical figure, one might say, that is only skin deep? In light of the highly charged metonymies of the Corpus Christi procession as the not-too-distant ancestors of the Godiva procession, it is difficult to see Godiva as an anti-metonymy, a signifier calling attention to its lack of signification.

The layers of meaning surrounding her, however, may still be ambiguous. After hitting on the effectiveness of the parody, the citizens are unlikely to have analyzed every implication of the elegant part-for-the-whole substitution. But like language itself the rhetoric of processions has a way of slipping beyond its prescribed limits. It is possible to suggest more ideals by which the Godiva of the procession, through design or not, functioned as the rhetorical vehicle. She could represent History, since Godgifu in 1043 founded the monastery that became the center of Coventry. She could also stand for Liberty (she frees the town from taxation) or Domestic Order (she fulfills her husband's demand), or Miracle (returning unseen) or even Salvation (combining mercy and a saving act). Cumulatively, her various roles function as a kind of metonymy to define Coventry itself. Similarly, the position of the Godiva rider within the Great Fair procession defines Godiva's function within a series of socially constructed roles, primarily within the order created by the craft guilds and the town officials. As Coventry's "patroness" surrounded by figures of male authority, she is the focal point of a great deal of civic pride and affection.

More than any of these functions, however, beyond the identities that can be linked specifically to Coventry, her nakedness defines her role as Erotic Display. Would anyone remember the story of Godiva if she lowered Coventry's taxes without taking off her clothes? The artificiality of her identity in the procession is illustrated by a detail from the record of 1678, which indicates that the son of James Swinnerton played the role of Godiva.[43] Thus the crowds were presented with the unlikely spectacle of a boy dressed up as a woman undressed. As counter-intuitive as this substitution may be, the purpose of the procession is not to provide the spectators with a real woman's body to view, but to provide a representation of erotic display. In public theater boys had already ceased playing the roles of women, so casting one as Godiva might have seemed anachronistic in 1678. Because actresses were engaged in a "low" occupation, they were already considered compromised as erotic displays and were available to be hired as Godiva impersonators. After 1678 there is no record of a boy playing the part again.

Not coincidentally, the period after the Restoration was marked by another kind of anxiety concerning dress. Sumptuary laws, which reached their greatest elaboration in Elizabeth's reign and which helped to prevent the upwardly mobile from overreaching their stations, had been summarily declared "repealed and void" in 1604 within a year of James's accession.[44] But after the Restoration social climbing was replaced by another source of anxiety: the scandal of women's fashions. At the beginning of the sixteenth century, sumptuary laws specified how low necklines could plunge by stipulating measurements to the collarbone. By the end of the sixteenth century and in the early seventeenth century, "elegant ladies' fashion featured a new low in extreme décolletage," in which "interest in the bosom demanded more exposure than compression; and the bosom began to look as if it might escape."[45]

The end of sumptuary laws did not signal the end of public proclamations about dress; they found different forms of expression. For example, a pamphlet entitled *A Just and Seasonable Reprehension of Naked Breasts and Shoulders*, translated from a French treatise "Written by a Grave and Learned Papist," was published in London in 1678 – the same year as the first official Godiva procession. A preface by Richard Baxter, a nonconformist theologian who, coincidentally, lived in Coventry during the Civil War, sets aside his religious differences with the author to urge it upon England's Protestants. The pamphlet condemns women who "appear with naked Breasts" not only at balls, but who "even come to triumph as it were over *Jesus Christ* himself, at the feet of his Altars."[46] Its obsession with the scandal of plunging necklines seems pathological (it goes on in relentless detail for 150 pages), but much of it is curiously relevant to the Godiva procession and legend. At times, as in the passage above, women "with naked Breasts" at the communion rail undermine the reverence due to the eucharistic body of Christ just as surely as a Godiva impersonator. In other passages that anticipate counter-arguments, it speculates about how a woman should respond to a coercive husband who compels her to go out in public dressed in a way that exposes too much of her body:

> we will suppose also that her husband should command her to go in publick with her naked neck, she ought to do so through pure obedience to make herself innocent; but she ought to do it with some secret repugnance, knowing the danger to which she exposes herself and those who behold her.[47]

She must obey her husband's command as long as she keeps her intentions pure and does what she can to limit the dangers. It reads almost as if the advice might be directed at Godiva for the way she should conduct herself on the ride that her husband forces upon her. The French origin of this pamphlet is enough to ensure that it was written without Godiva in mind, but the pairing of the consecrated host with a woman's exposed body, the husband's coercion, the woman's "secret repugnance," and the danger posed "to those who behold her" invokes issues that are central to the legend and the procession. Both the pamphlet and the legend address anxieties about sexuality and social control in the latter seventeenth century, though one with pious earnestness and the other in festive defiance. Such concerns about women's fashion and social control may help explain the timing of the Godiva legend's popularity beyond Warwickshire. Once an erotic identity was elaborated for her, Lady Godiva was poised for wider circulation.

The surest marker of that identity is the figure of Peeping Tom – or more precisely the nature of his gaze. Here it helps to keep in mind another difference from the earlier Corpus Christi procession, but it could just as well be any public procession where a crowd gathers to watch. The gazing is collective, with everyone aware that everyone else is looking at whatever is on display, whether that is the host in a monstrance, the person of a monarch, or, for that matter, a play on stage, a marching band, or a criminal in chains. Processions are held in city streets precisely to enable as much collective viewing as possible. Even under more ordinary circumstances pedestrians are rarely expected to avert their eyes on city streets, and they may feel uncomfortable chancing upon, for example, a display of physical intimacy.

The obverse of the public collective gaze is Peeping Tom's voyeurism, which not only violates norms of privacy but is surreptitious precisely so that no one else knows that he is doing it. It is not enough that he conceal his gaze from Godiva herself, he must conceal it from everyone. Because voyeurism is transgressive by definition, it arouses guilt, and thus Tom's punishment can seem somehow appropriate, however disproportionate it is. Voyeurism involves a gaze from one enclosed space to another, typically from a hiding place into a private room. Peeping Tom, on the other hand, gazes from a private room into the most public of spaces. Why should he avert his eyes? Godiva is not only on the street, but her elevated position on a horse puts her more prominently on display. One way of interpreting the edict introduced into the legend is as an attempt to extend Godiva's private chamber from her house throughout the streets of the town, but however effective the edict was imagined to be, it runs counter to deeply entrenched assumptions about the difference between public and private space. No version of the legend asserts that the edict eliminates her sense of shame, as if she could ride through the streets with her privacy assured (though some are silent on this point).

The later Godiva processions overturn the distinction not by intruding the private into the public, but by festively abolishing the separation between the two. It is partly a function of genre. The re-enactment invokes a rhetoric of processions, which is different from the literary tale. Just as the Godiva of literature never escapes a sense of shame, however, the Godiva of the processions is never unequivocally transformed into a public spectacle for collective gazing. There remains a residue of voyeurism, so that the procession becomes the occasion for individuals in the crowd to imagine themselves as voyeurs, as if thousands of Peeping Toms spilled out of their hiding places and overflowed the streets. A 1767 poem by the Warwickshire native Richard Jago speaks deprecatingly of the "cavalcade" in Coventry:

> Made yearly to Godiva's deathless praise,
> While gaping crowds around her pageant throng,
> With prying look and stupid wonderment . . .[48]

Few crowds gathered to witness a civic procession would be described with the crude lasciviousness of "gaping" and "prying" looks. Jago uses the event to draw a distinction between their gross improprieties and his own more refined perspective. But the distinction between high and low dissolves with alarming ease (later in the poem) in his narration of Godiva's heroic ride. As with the earliest accounts from St Albans', Jago's narrative voice presents the ride as something shameful to Godiva and forbidden to the town's citizens ("Prostrate to earth th' astonished vassals bow"), but at the same time it invites the gaze to linger on her "naked beauty," "her dishevelled hair," and "her beauteous limbs," which is exactly what the "gaping" and "prying" crowds in Coventry are chastised for doing.[49]

Jago's description of the crowd in Coventry may not be far off the mark. The behavior of the participants in nineteenth-century processions demonstrates in various ways how the Godiva-for-a-day never quite completed the transformation into an aestheticized spectacle.[50] There are stories that the crowd's anticipation would be whipped up by rumors each year that the woman impersonating Godiva would wear little or nothing – that she would *really* be naked. With or without such rumors, the crowds were said to exceed 50,000 in the nineteenth century. In 1842 (the year Tennyson's famous "Lady Godiva" was published), the woman on horseback "was so close an imitation of the celebrated Countess that she nearly caused a riot among the crowd, who were all anxious for a closer view." Two years later a minister thunders in a Coventry pamphlet:

> But what was there to make the procession so attractive? There was a *strumpet*, she was the attraction. But what could attract so many thousands to look at a strumpet? What but the expectation of seeing her *naked*? Such alas is the state of moral feeling in the city of Coventry, in the middle of the nineteenth century.[51]

An aspiring American poet by the name of Henry Wadsworth Longfellow recorded his disapproval in more restrained language when his young gentleman's tour of England took him to Coventry the day after the 1829 procession. "The custom of riding the naked woman through the streets is still preserved," he reflects in his journal, "and some wench from Birmingham generally officiates in flesh coloured tights. O tempora! O mores!"[52]

The "naked" woman wore more than flesh-colored tights. A local account of the 1829 procession that young Longfellow just missed records that the impersonator also wore a tight-fitting linen dress, "which was relieved with a variety of gay ornaments, and a long gauze scarf suspended from her hair. She was also furnished with long ringlets, which flowed over the greater part of her body, and with a large bunch of flowers to complete the equipment."[53] As Longfellow suggests, the Godiva was usually an actress hired from another city and paid a significant sum for her efforts. According to some accounts the actresses were offered drinks by inn-keepers along the way, which they sometimes accepted, with unfortunate results by the end. Town officials also showed signs of anxiety by passing legislation that restricted the procession and by surrounding Godiva with representatives of law enforcement. The order of procession in 1764, for example, shows Lady Godiva preceded by the high constable and followed by two bailiffs and two sergeants. By 1809 the official presence had increased, so that Lady Godiva was preceded by the high constable, flanked by the city crier and beadle (dressed in the colors of the bishop), and followed by the mayor's crier, the city bailiffs, and the city macebearers. By 1826, her escort had added the mayor himself, aldermen, sheriffs, the common council, chamberlains, and wardens.[54] Was Godiva's erotic display so provocative that it that demanded the protection of so many figures of male authority?

It is easy to dismiss the account of the mock procession quoted at the beginning of this chapter. It is, after all, a second-hand account of doubtful authenticity, uncertain date, and with an obvious bias. But it is worth attending to as an interpretive catalyst in thinking about the legend's reception, because, spurious or not, it draws together many of salient characteristics of Godiva's progress from the Middle Ages up through the eighteenth century. It shows how the drama of the legend translates so well into the drama of a procession. It draws together religious and civic conflicts from Coventry's history in a tension that can still be sensed. And it offers a dynamic way to think about the difference between the collective and the voyeuristic gaze. Coventry's voyeur for the ages, Peeping Tom, is the subject of the next chapter.

Chapter 4

Peeping Tom

Over the years "Peeping Tom" has become such a familiar expression that many people are surprised to learn it arose as a by-product of the Godiva legend. Although a voyeur character was not added for several centuries after the earliest St. Albans chronicles, Peeping Tom and Lady Godiva have since developed into complementary opposites in so many ways that each has become a means of defining the other. He is hidden while she is on public display; his gaze is active and she is its passive object; his social position is low and hers is high; he is wicked and she is virtuous; his sexuality is questioned while hers is affirmed; his conscience feels guilt where she feels shame; he is punished and she is rewarded. Their pairing anticipates Sigmund Freud's clinical definitions of scopophilia and exhibitionism in terms of one another so well that he almost seems to have Peeping Tom in mind for the former and Lady Godiva for the latter. Only in recent years has Peeping Tom become extricated from the Godiva legend to the extent that it is possible to mention one without calling to mind the other.

In some of the early versions of the legend the townspeople do not look upon the naked Godiva either because of divine intervention or because of a virtuous exercise of self-restraint. Consequently the reader is the only one who could be said to assume the role of a voyeur, and the narrative's rhetoric creates the condition for it. By the time of Richard of Grafton's 1569 paraphrase of the lost medieval chronicle of Prior Geoffrey, however, this state of affairs changed. Before her ride, according to Grafton, Godiva makes a special appeal to the "Magistrates and rulers of the sayde City of Couentrie," as if a miracle or self-restraint is no longer sufficient. The officials proclaim a "streight commaundement" that everyone shut themselves in their houses and not look out under penalty of "a great paine."[1] A few decades later, the

ballad by Thomas Deloney incorporates the addition of an official proclamation, and the ballad's popularity made this new twist to the story
increasingly common in later accounts. In some of these Leofric himself
issues the proclamation. The appearance of a character who defies the
edict is almost an inevitability.

One of the earliest references to a voyeur is from a journal kept by
three soldiers of Norwich during a tour of England in 1634. In the account of their visit to Coventry it offers a summary of the legend, in
which Godiva had "[t]o ride naked openly, at high Noone day, through
the City, vpon a milke white steed, which she willingly perform'd." The
passage then ends, "It may bee very well discuss'd heere, whether
[Leofric's] hatred, or [Godiva's] Loue exceeded,"

> Her fayre long hayre did much offend
> the wantons glancing Eye.[2]

Though written as prose in the published edition of the diary, the last
two lines have the metrical rhythm of a ballad stanza, which, unless it is
a lost stanza from Deloney, is possibly a snatch of an unknown ballad
jotted down from memory. One can only guess what her hair did to
"offend" anyone. If "wanton" refers to a Peeping Tom figure, it would
be the earliest reference, though within a few decades of 1634 the voy-
eur-figure is attested elsewhere. But "wanton" could also refer to Leofric,
if the soldiers knew a version of the legend like Grafton's, in which
Leofric relishes the thought of his wife riding naked in the public streets.

The soldiers' recollection of the old legend is prompted by their visit
to a "fayre large Hall" (probably St. Mary's Hall) near the cathedral,
where they examine a painting of Godiva. The upper end of the hall,
they observe, is

> adorn'd with rich Hangings, and all about with fayre Pictures, one more
> especially of a noble Lady, whose memory they haue cause not to forget,
> for that shee purchas'd and redeem'd their lost infring'd Liberties, and
> Freedomes, and obtain'd remission of heauy Tributes impos'd vpon them,
> by vndertaking a hard, and vnseemely taske.[3]

The painting of Lady Godiva that they describe is most likely one that
dates from 1586 (plate 2). It shows a bearded man looking out an up-
stairs window from a building in the background. In the foreground
Godiva rides side-saddle through the empty city streets. For centuries
the presence of this onlooker had been obscured and forgotten because

of varnish and grime covering the canvas. It may have been lost to view as early as 1681, when a copy of the older painting was made which lacked the bearded man. He did not re-emerge until 1976, when a cleaning of the painting uncovered him again. At such an early date as 1586, the bearded onlooker was most likely placed there as Leofric observing his wife on her ride, not as an anonymous voyeur. But because his identity as Leofric is not obvious, later visitors (such as the soldiers) may have identified it as a citizen who looks surreptitiously on Godiva's nakedness.[4] Indeed the wording of the soldiers' journal leaves it unclear whether "wanton" refers to the figure in the painting or to a character in the ballad they quote.

In one sense the ambiguous identity of the unknown onlooker is entirely appropriate, because the roles of Leofric the villain and of the citizen-voyeur, which become conventionalized at roughly the same time, seem to be two sides of a kind of male sexual fantasy. Insofar as Leofric circulates his wife's body throughout the town in a tightly controlled demonstration of power, he desires to display what he possesses without relinquishing it. The voyeur's intrusive gaze, on the other hand, is motivated by a desire to possess what he cannot have.[5]

Eventually the shady citizen-voyeur began to assume more of an identity. By the middle of the seventeenth century the character was established well enough that a wooden statue representing him was erected in a window overlooking Coventry's streets. A visitor to Coventry in 1659 "was told by one of the citizens that the man would look at Godiva out of that window, and for that he was stricken dead."[6] The instantaneous punishment (either death or blinding) quickly becomes established as an essential part of the legend. Its supernatural quality suggests the working of a transcendent justice and divine favor for Godiva so that readers rarely pause to question its harshness. But in most societies voyeurism is a minor misdemeanor if it is a crime at all. It becomes a capital crime only in legends such as Actaeon and Diana or Susannah and the Elders, where the punishment's severity and divine intervention elevates the action beyond history into the realm of mythical archetype. Blindness too has a broad symbolism appropriate to the erotics of the legend, because it is a substitute for castration in both classical myth (for example Oedipus) and Freudian psychoanalysis.

The Coventry Peeping Tom statue, which dates from around 1500, survives today (plate 3). Though it is now stripped down to the oak, over the years it had accumulated many layers of paint. At some early point its two arms were removed for better maneuvering in and out of

Plate 2 Adam van Noort, *Lady Godiva*, 1586

windows, and parts of it have been gouged away, perhaps by souvenir-seekers. Sources extending back to 1765 record expenses for a wig and painting of the statue to prepare it for the Great Show Fair. The presumed seventeenth-century origin for its role in the procession helps to explain the persistence of the tradition of dressing it up in a Restoration-era costume, complete with wig. In a diary entry for 1792 Lord Torrington writes "Close to our inn, the King's Head, is the figure of Peeping Tom, projecting from the front of a house, dated 1700; and, after the fashion of the day, he is equipped in a large laced Hat, and a full wig."[7] Thus a statue from the turn of the sixteenth-century was given a seventeenth-century costume which it wore well into the eighteenth century and beyond.

In literature the figure at first had no identity other than as a citizen-voyeur. A printing of Deloney's ballad from 1723 paraphrases an account derived from the St. Albans chronicles, but then goes on to say "at Coventry they tell us another Sort of a Story." Godiva commands that all doors and windows be shut up and that no one be permitted to look out. "And a poor Taylor, who would needs be peeping, was struck blind." It leaves the impression that the blinding of the tailor was common knowledge in Coventry.[8] As a tailor he would conveniently be equipped with an awl to bore a viewing hole, but the occupation would be appropriate for other reasons as well. Proverbially, tailors were thought to be less than fully men even to the point of suggesting their emasculation ("Nine tailors make the man").[9] So, for example, when a tailor in a fairy tale accomplishes something heroic, his deficient manhood throws the magical transformation into greater relief. In addition, the tailor's business of making clothes, in contrast to Godiva's nakedness, may have added to the thematic appeal.

About the time that he is provided with an occupation, the voyeur is given a name. He is called "the fellow who peeped" in the journal of a visiting clergyman in 1690, and Daniel Defoe, using almost identical language, speaks of "the poor fellow that peep'd out of the window to see her . . . looking out of a Garret in the High Street of the City."[10] The 1723 printing of Deloney's ballad says that the wooden statue is called "the Peeper" by the locals in Coventry. By the mid-eighteenth century the name Peeping Tom is used in ways that assume it is already widely known. Coventry town records for 1765, for example, list expenses for "Peeping Tom" and five years later the name appears in a mock-heroic poem by Edward Thompson called "The Meretriciad":

> The world must stare, two Heroines to see,
> Fighting for Peeping Tom of Coventry.
>   (lines 680–1)

As the title suggests, Thompson modeled his poem after Alexander Pope's "Dunciad," using elevated language to parody a trivial subject.

If a mock-religious procession making use of a Godiva impersonator took place before the town-sponsored procession of 1678 (as suggested in the previous chapter), it would coincide with several quirks in the evolution of Peeping Tom. The first literary and historical references to a voyeur antedate 1678. Perhaps the character was not pure invention. Let us suppose that a man impersonating the voyeur mysteriously died after playing the part in a procession. A superstition arising from the death would explain why there is no record of a citizen playing the part even in the first town-sponsored procession in 1678. Given the range of characters who annually marched, and given Tom's

Plate 3 Peeping Tom effigy, ca. 1500

importance in the legend from the mid-1600s, the tradition of representing him as a statue leaning out a window needs some explanation. Why is the role of Tom never played by an impersonator like that of Godiva? Because of the procession's potential for religious parody, a superstition like the one described in the last chapter might inspire considerable fear. Thus the wooden statue, put to this use before 1659, fits into this hypothetical chain of events as a safe substitute. If so, perhaps the punishment for the voyeur was added to the legend because an impersonator suddenly died after an early mock procession. Most studies of the Godiva legend reasonably assume that the procession took its form under the influence of written and oral accounts of the legend, but the direction of influence could conceivably switch. Local events may have influenced the story's plot. In this case, the shocking death of a performer might have found its way back into the legend as a voyeur who was punished for his transgression during Godiva's supposed eleventh-century ride. Whatever the causes and sequence, by the time the legend emerged after the Restoration the role of Peeping Tom had become indispensable.

The incorporation of Peeping Tom into the plot does more than foreground the dynamics of the transgressive gaze. When he appears in literary works the voyeur assumes the always useful function of scapegoat. In Richard Jago's Edge Hill (1767) for example, Leofric, after contemplating Godiva's "nicest sense of shame," commands her to ride in "naked beauty" through the town, exposed to the "gazing slaves" who inhabit it.

> At length her female fears
> Gave way, and sweet humanity prevail'd.
> Reluctant, but resolv'd, the matchless fair
> Gives all her naked beauty to the Sun;
> Then mounts her milk-white steed, and, through the streets,
> Rides fearless; her dishevell'd hair a veil!
> That o'er her beauteous limbs luxuriant flow'd.[11]

Continuing a pattern established in the earliest versions of the St. Albans chroniclers, Jago's reader assumes the perspective of a voyeur, when Godiva "gives all her naked beauty to the Sun." And the luxuriant hair conceals at the same time that it invites the reader to imagine her "beauteous limbs." The justification for exposing herself to the shame of the ride is her virtuous compassion for the suffering citizens, her "sweet humanity," in contrast to her husband's callous disregard. Such moralistic beauty-worshiping from a privileged perspective contrasts with the other voyeur:

> . . . one prying slave! who fondly hop'd,
> With venial curiosity, to gaze
> On such a wondrous dame.

His transgressive gazing earns him a terrible if unspecified punishment (we can assume blindness), so that he becomes "a spectacle abhorred." But more crucially for literary retellings of the legend, the guilt of voyeurism is transferred to him, so that the reader can continue to gaze on such a wondrous dame with venial curiosity – and with impunity. The narrator and reader are no less voyeuristic than Tom. Why are they no more sympathetic to him? To acquiesce in such a harsh punishment for such a trivial crime is to capitalize on the convenience of Peeping Tom as a scapegoat. How different are the motivations, finally, between the Peeping Tom, the reader, and the "gaping crowds" that gathered annually for the Coventry processions?

It is helpful to recall the mock procession, where both the voyeuristic and the collective forms of viewing are produced: on one hand the "Merry Andrew" on a pageant wagon who looks out of a window "with profane jests" and on the other the crowd on the street who witness the spectacle. The pageant wagon stages the private space of a house's interior within a public arena. Did the voyeur in the pageant wagon have the same scapegoat function as the voyeur in literature, and allow the crowds to look on with impunity? Probably not. Part of the carnivalesque humor of a Godiva procession derives from the crowd recognizing itself using both the voyeuristic and collective gaze. For everyone to see himself as both solitary and a part of a crowd elicits a kind of double consciousness. Yet the laughter may have had an anxious edge to it if the wooden statue was first pressed into service to protect the onlookers from the divine retribution they were not sure could not happen. So Peeping Tom serves as a substitute in two different ways: in literature, he becomes a scapegoat to bear guilt; in the procession, he becomes a talisman to stave off retribution (as the last chapter argued). Only later would the statue become a mere prop.

Literature and processions are only two genres that manipulate the voyeuristic perspective inherent in the legend. Painting and sculpture also shape the distinction between viewer and voyeur. For example, Edwin Landseer, one of Queen Victoria's favorite painters, exhibited *Lady Godiva's Prayer* at the Royal Academy in 1866 (plate 4), where it met with a cool critical reception. F. G. Stephens, for one, dismissed it as "unfortunate." Earlier that year, however, the queen saw it on a visit to Landseer's studio and was sufficiently impressed to write about it to her daughter:

I think you might like to hear what I saw at Landseer's the other day.

Such beautiful unfinished things. A "Lady Godiva" most charmingly treated, on a dun pony (of course, nude but, so simply arranged – you see her back and she has her arms outstretched, offering up a prayer to be supported in this terrible ordeal), an old Duenna standing by, closing her eyes.[12]

Although she protests too much about the modest state of Godiva's nakedness, Victoria's description is fairly accurate. While art critics since Stephens have continued to see in it signs of Landseer's diminishing skills, Victoria's opinion was closer to the public reception. Landseer was the most popular painter of his day, and the year after his death in 1873 the painting fetched an impressive £3,360 at auction.

Landseer's addition of the servant allows him a composition that includes the two most typical postures for Godiva, the gaze uplifted as if inspired by a higher purpose, and the gaze averted in shame. The vertical axis marked by the steeple and continuing down to the spaniel's snout divides the painting into two parts. On one side are the horse and servant who cannot bear to look. Godiva seems to be the only one indifferent to her nakedness. As Anne Hollander observes of unclothed figures in art:

> Sexual messages are always delivered by the image of an unclothed body; and even more intense ones must then necessarily be conveyed by a bare body shown in the company of a covered one . . . because the dressed figure is usually perceived as aware of the undressed one or vice versa–or else the spectator is the voyeur, and that produces the eroticism by itself.[13]

While the closed eyes of Landseer's servant signal a pained awareness of Godiva's nakedness, it is more than a gesture of shame on behalf of her mistress. It also attempts to mitigate the guilt of our (the viewer's) voyeurism, not through a Peeping Tom-type scapegoating but by an empathy in which we momentarily identify with the servant's inability to look. In the other half of the painting Godiva's gesture and the flowing lines of her body and not quite unbound hair finally command the viewer's attention, but the mediating role of the servant, who directly faces the viewer, allows Landseer's painting to stage the dynamics of Godiva's shame and the voyeur's guilt.

The servant's age, clothing, and ruffled collar call to mind the portraits of the time of Rembrandt, and the figure thus seems oddly anachronistic for a medieval subject that usually called for the Gothic or classical

Plate 4 Sir Edwin Landseer, *Lady Godiva's Prayer*, ca. 1865

style in the mid-nineteenth century. The evocation of seventeenth-century genre painting side by side with Landseer's trademark spaniel and
doves at the bottom may be hints for the viewer to look at the composition according to the conventions of realistic portraiture. Godiva is
not riding in the never-never land of medievalist fantasies nor in the

timeless past of classicism, but in a more proximate, historically accessible past. Its realism may signal that Landseer wanted the viewer to accept the authenticity of the legend.

While artists, writers, and Coventry's citizens have demonstrated a sophisticated understanding of Peeping Tom's voyeurism, the rise of psychoanalysis at the turn of the twentieth century has led to more theoretical insights. Sigmund Freud, for example, was acquainted with the Godiva legend and used it on one occasion to illustrate the psychically induced disturbances of the sense of sight. It is customary to assume that a person in Godiva's exposed state experiences shame; a person like Peeping Tom who transgresses a moral prohibition feels guilt. Freud sees both shame and guilt afflicting the voyeur or scopophiliac. He presupposes that the voyeur has already overcome guilt – otherwise there would be no activity to analyze – and shame is the remaining deterrence. "The force which opposes scopophilia, but which may be overridden by it," writes Freud, ". . . is shame."[14] It differs from guilt, which remains internalized with the individual, in that it has an essential social component. Shame cannot arise outside the context of a community. It accompanies the anxiety of being caught in the act.

In a famous illustration of this principle Jean-Paul Sartre imagines, "Here I am bent over the keyhole; suddenly I hear a footstep. I shudder as a wave of shame sweeps over me. Somebody has seen me. I straighten up. My eyes run over the deserted corridor. It was a false alarm. I breathe a sigh of relief."[15] The guilt of the voyeur is superseded by shame, which prompts the subsequent realization of oneself as an object in the eyes of another, even when there is no "other" there, when the alarm is false. A gazer-at-the-keyhole who is indifferent to the shame of being caught in the act would presumably no longer be a voyeur, and indifference could come about only when guilt is absent.

Unlike Sartre's existential peeper, though, the Peeping Tom of the traditional legend does not experience a wave of shame as described by Sartre because he never hears footsteps; he is unobserved by Godiva and the town's citizens. His blinding (or death) comes without warning, as if the mysterious power that punishes has him under its own hidden surveillance. He does not escape the effects of shame altogether, however. To Freud his blinding is the symbolic equivalent of castration (compare Oedipus's blindness), but it also disfigures him with a permanent sign of shame within the community.

For the most part, though, the legend seems to suspend Lady Godiva and Peeping Tom in uncomplicated states, as if they are part allegory and part icon. Public nakedness, the attitude of abject shame that Godiva is forced to assume, is so fundamental that it remains a staple of anxiety dreams. Yet she is never touched, never possessed, only exposed. Aside from the reader/viewer, she is seen only by Peeping Tom, who does little more than surreptitiously observe a naked body. The very simplicity of their roles in a human activity as basic as voyeurism give them an extensive explanatory power usually associated with myth. The universality helps explain how "Peeping Tom" has moved from a bit part in a Coventry's processions to a commonplace expression in the English language.

Chapter 5

Godiva Domesticated

In 1856 Queen Victoria gave an oil painting of herself on horseback to her husband Albert as a present on his forty-seventh birthday. For his next birthday she gave him a small silver statue of a nude Lady Godiva on horseback.[1] Since Victoria was fond of giving Albert images of herself for his birthday, it would be unfair to read this particular sequence too literally – as if, for example, there were a simple equivalence between the uniformed Victoria in one and the naked Godiva in the other. Birthday gifts are rarely given with such deliberate and consistent calculation from one year to the next. Nevertheless her choices reveal some things about the way Victoria viewed herself in relation to her husband and her larger public duties at a stage in her life when she had become firmly established in each role.

Victoria's decision to commission the statue raises questions about the significance she saw beyond the object's aesthetic appeal. By the mid-nineteenth century the Godiva legend was so well known that any artistic representation would convey a range of cultural values. For example, the Victorian version of Godiva was ready – however reluctantly – to forgo the private role society expected of women and to risk public exposure. Godiva was also such an advocate for the common people that she was willing to sacrifice herself for them, yet she emerged from her ordeal with her nobility intact and even enhanced. Even though Victoria had a general fondness for nudes in other works that she acquired for Osborne House, her gift also had personal connotations as a private erotic token between wife and husband.

But the statue may have been a tactful attempt to mitigate a marital issue of another sort. Less than two months earlier, Victoria had used royal letters patent to confer on Albert the title "Prince Consort of the United Kingdom of Great Britain and Ireland," which finally affirmed his legal status in the hierarchy of the royal family. She would have preferred a parliamentary bill to confer the title but was advised against it because Albert, despite years of public service, remained the target of xenophobic mistrust among members of Parliament and the press. To Albert's mind, the honor should have come at the time of his marriage, seventeen years earlier.[2] Again the legend behind the statue is relevant: Godiva's ride is, among other things, an act of submission to her husband. Although today the ride is sometimes seen as a gesture of defiance, the nineteenth-century version of the story ends with Godiva returning meekly to her husband after fulfilling the conditions he stipulates. Yet she also succeeds in getting public policy changed. Thus Victoria's gift may have signified – almost apologetically – that she remained Albert's dutiful wife despite their unequal stations and the burdensome obligations that drew her out of their home to engage publicly with the concerns of the larger society.

Beyond all such speculative interpretations, however, the gift shows how domesticated the Godiva legend had become in England by the nineteenth century. Throughout Victoria's reign Godiva was increasingly apotheosized in art and literature, at a time when, paradoxically, historians had affirmed that the story of her ride was fictitious. Part of the appeal was the widespread romanticization of the Middle Ages known today as medievalism, but it was more than that. Like Victoria, growing numbers of women activists and writers turned to the legendary Godiva for inspiration.

The public/private tension signaled in Victoria's choice of subject for the statue resonated in the larger society in two ways. For the first time in English history, a significant part of the population – the growing middle class – could be assured of physical privacy at home. It was especially significant to married couples who could afford houses with the architectural separation of rooms to sleep, bathe, and dress without fear of intrusion. Today the availability of bedrooms and bathrooms is widely taken for granted, but before the nineteenth century only a small percentage of the population in England and Europe had the means to escape the usual condition, in which any number of people would be crowded together. Privacy might be attempted by a curtain, darkness, a blanket or some other unreliable means.[3] While the notional distinction between public and private has always existed, for most of world history (not merely Western), life indoors has put people in such close proximity with one another that privacy has been compromised from the start.

If the means for physical privacy at home first became widely available in middle-class England of the nineteenth century, the timing helps explain the Victorians' fascination with the Godiva legend. In any period the appearance of an aristocrat undressed in public would be a humiliating violation of decent behavior, but the naked body *by itself* would have less shock value when secure privacy was a privilege enjoyed by relatively few. In Godiva's case what would be more significant is the deliberate choice to renounce or jeopardize her privacy, since she was one of the few people in her society capable of preserving it and whose class status in part depended on keeping herself physically separate. Because of the newly secured sense of privacy in Victorian England, hand in glove with the importance of social respectability and individual sensibility, a deliberate display of nakedness in public could be received as more scandalous, more electrifying than it would be in a society where occasional violations might be endured as a passing embarrassment. Thus in Victorian literature the need for a scapegoat figure to insulate the reader from guilt becomes more urgent, and in the Coventry processions the Godiva display attracts both larger crowds and fiercer denunciations.

Another, related issue raised by Queen Victoria's gift to Albert is the increasing idealization of the domestic/private world reserved for women and the business/public world for men. Nevertheless, women could assume public responsibilities, just as men had a role in the home, which John Ruskin formulates with elegant symmetry:

> Now the man's work for his own home is, as has been said, to secure its maintenance, progress, and defense; the woman's to secure its order, comfort, and loveliness.
>
> Expand both these functions. The man's duty, as a member of a commonwealth, is to assist in the maintenance, in the advance, in the defense of the state. The woman's duty, as a member of the commonwealth, is to assist in the ordering, in the comforting, and in the beautiful adornment of the state.

But when she ventures outside the gates of home, "order is more difficult, distress more imminent, loveliness more rare."[4] Ruskin's ideal was to urge middle-class women to pursue philanthropy, which was one of the few avenues of public activity open to them. And while he does not invoke Godiva, his contemporaries turned to the legend because it en-

acts the precariousness of a woman's attempt to bring about public order and comfort, and her imperiled loveliness only adds to the aesthetic
appeal. In short the legend became a Victorian model of a woman's
passage from the domestic to the public world and (conversely) its re-
warding capacity to bring about social change. Queen Victoria's involvement with the public world was substantial, of course, but her gift to
Albert subordinates it and signals her sympathy for society's traditional
gendered roles. Godiva's journey from her home to the city streets and
back again was a model not only for the queen but for growing numbers of middle-class women.

Perhaps no work, historical or literary, did more to domesticate the
legend in this period than Alfred Tennyson's "Godiva," published in his
Poems of 1842. Though it fell out of favor in the twentieth century (so
that, for example, it is rarely anthologized), "Godiva" was consistently
singled out in reviews immediately after publication and even printed
in its entirety in several of them.[5] Its appeal to the reviewers was not
simply a function of the sensational subject matter or even its moderate
length (seventy-nine lines), but rather in the way it reads contemporary themes into its historical subject. In addition to the public/private
tensions discussed above, Tennyson points to the underlying anxieties
behind the rapid industrialization of the nineteenth century and its ex-
ploitation of the working class.[6] The opening proem gestures toward
these concerns with a disarming casualness:

> I waited for the train at Coventry;
> I hung with grooms and porters on the bridge,
> To watch the three tall spires; and there I shaped
> The city's ancient legend into this

The train service passing through Coventry from London to Birmingham had started only two years before Tennyson visited the city in
1840, so to invoke it in the first line is to single out a novelty in the
urban landscape. As the engine of industry, the train is set against the
backdrop of the medieval steeples, which evoke a simpler age of spiritual and political idealism. In mingling with grooms and porters, the
poet shows how he, like Godiva, can sympathize with the city's working class. Even the colloquial verb he uses, "hung with," shortens the
distance between poet and laborers.[7] The suggested connections between the present and past are more explicit in the opening lines of the
poem proper, which question the Victorian cult of progress:

> Not only we, the latest seed of Time,
> New men, that in the flying of a wheel
> Cry down the past, not only we, that prate
> Of rights and wrongs, have loved the people well,
> And loathed to see them overtax'd . . .

To identify the "New men" merely with "we, the latest seed of Time" is to deny the notion of moral improvement over history: seeds reproduce the same plant generation after generation. (Darwin's *Origin of Species* was seventeen years away.) But worse than stasis, the opening counterbalances industrial progress with an ethical regression from effective action to prating of rights and wrongs. The steam engine as a tangible sign of industrialization, "the flying of a wheel," threatens to obliterate history. As if the tracks were a time line, it "Cr[ies] down the past," both in the sense of overwhelming it with mechanical noise and trivializing it with the semantic emptiness of steam. The tracks virtually mark out a chronology that has no destination and no meaningful intervals, except perhaps the stop at Coventry. Tennyson identifies himself with the "New men" who love and sympathize with the people but are incapable of heroic action like Godiva's. Yet as a poet he accepts the moral imperative to "shape" the legend so that words might inspire deeds again. By not plunging directly into the mythic past and by introducing his subject through contemporary concerns Tennyson seeks to avoid the escapism often associated with the fantasies of Victorian medievalism.

Tennyson may well have believed the legend's authenticity. He made use of the St. Albans account in Dugdale's *Antiquities of Warwickshire,* but it is likely he consulted other sources because certain details, such as the herald proclaiming the ride through the town and the blinding of the peeping tailor, are not in Dugdale.[8] By the nineteenth century the legend was available in so many versions that tracing Tennyson's sources can become pointless. All of the major details in the poem were readily available or were commonly known. Yet he brings out the melodrama even more than the broadsheet ballads: the villainous Leofric as compassionless as his dogs; mothers who bring their starving children and clamor, "If we pay, we starve!"; Godiva's sympathy for the people contesting with her shrinking modesty.

The social dynamics, however, are overshadowed by the erotic imagery of the poem. The guilt of voyeurism has been transferred to "one low churl, compact of thankless earth," whose eyes shrivel and fall out as he attempts to look upon Godiva's body. His punishment enables the reader to gaze with impunity as she rides on "clothed in chastity." The displacement of guilt extends to the deserted streets, where even animals and architectural details become voyeurs:

> The little wide-mouthed heads upon the spout
> Had cunning eyes to see: the barking cur
> Made her cheek flame: her palfrey's footfall shot
> Light horrors through her pulses: the blind walls
> Were full of chinks and holes; and overhead
> Fantastic gables, crowding, stared

Though the walls are "blind," the "chinks and holes" conceal *and* enable furtive viewing (compare a hunter's blind), which add to her horrors and heighten her sense of shame. By participating vicariously in this transgression the reader becomes a voyeur to the extent that one wonders whether Tennyson's Godiva is the champion of the oppressed or yet another object of male desire.[9]

One of the characteristic accomplishments of Tennyson's poem is the sophisticated way he allows Godiva to be both a champion and a victim at the same time. More than any other version of the legend his poem articulates a number of contraries that have always been part of it but are usually subordinated or ignored, and it does so in a way that each element coexists without canceling its opposite. Some of these binaries have already been mentioned in various contexts. Tennyson uses the Middle Ages to question modern virtues without escapist fantasies. Godiva is an aristocrat who identifies with the common people. The town is simultaneously crowded and empty. Her ride is an unsteady intrusion of the private into the public. She is both erotic and modest; both brave and fearful; both scandalous and innocent; both victimized and heroic; both assertive and manipulated; both defiant and submissive; both clothed (in hair, "in chastity") and unclothed; both seen and unseen. Even readers participate in these binaries to the extent that they are and are not voyeurs.

In a lengthy review of *Poems*, Leigh Hunt singled out "Morte d'Arthur" and "Godiva" as the two poems that "Mr. Tennyson thinks his best" in part because each is framed by a contemporary setting that Hunt considers a kind of rhetorical special pleading or (as he puts it) "literary dandyism, or fine-gentlemanism, or fastidiousness, or whatever he may *not* be pleased to call it."[10] Hunt sees Tennyson's invocation of the "grooms and porters" as a sign of condescension – "contempt" is the word he uses – because it is a contrived intrusion that distracts from Godiva's idealized heroism. He elaborates:

> The feelings of the heroine's heart ought to have been more spoken of, and those of the good people inside the houses, who did not think of "peeping," like the rascally tailor, but wept, and prayed, and loved the unseen angel that was going along. This would have been the way to do honour to the glorious Coventry heroine; and this is what few could have done better than Mr. Tennyson.[11]

Hunt could be an astute critic, but here he fails to realize that Tennyson was attempting something more ambitious than a rascally tailor peeping at a glorious angel. Despite its paternalistic tone, Hunt's lengthy review still betrays an admiration for the poet's emerging talents. To call "Godiva" one of the poems that Tennyson "thinks his best" is to reveal Hunt's own high estimate of it. He singles out as "the best passage" the dramatic exchange where Godiva pleads for the people only to be toyed with and spurned by Leofric, "ending with a truly Homeric bit of human animal painting":

> She told him of their tears,
> And prayed him, "If they pay this tax, they starve."
> Whereat he stared, replying, half-amazed,
> "you would not let your little finger ache
> For such as *these*?" – "But I would die," said she.
> He laughed, and swore by Peter and by Paul:
> Then filliped at the diamond in her ear:
> "Oh ay, ay, ay, you talk!" – "Alas!" she said,
> "But prove me what it is I would not do."
> And from a heart as rough as Esau's hand,
> He answered, "Ride you naked through the town,
> And I repeal it"; and nodding, as in scorn,
> He parted, with great strides among his dogs.
>
> (lines 19–31)

In contrast to Godiva's selfless idealism, Leofric's identity is defined by a crass materialism which makes Godiva as much a possession of his as the diamond in her ear. Her piety contrasts with his swearing by Peter and Paul and the invocation of Esau. But the melodrama that Hunt found so appealing is precisely the kind of saccharine excess that makes this passage something of an embarrassment to later tastes.

Hunt goes on to flatter Tennyson by calling him "a kind of philosophical Keats," and predicts that his best poems in the future will show "a mixture of thought and feeling, more abundant in the former respect than Keats, and more pleasurable and luxuriant in the latter than Wordsworth."[12] Although this invocation of the masters is a compliment of the highest order, it reveals Hunt's affinity with their Romantic agenda. His specific criticisms of the contemporary frames for "Godiva" and "Morte d'Arthur" are motivated by a preference for poetry that idealizes the Middle Ages, like Keats's surrealistic "La Belle Dame Sans Merci" (first published in Hunt's *Indicator* in 1821). His main disappointment is that Tennyson is not more of a Romantic.

Hunt had already taken up the subject of Lady Godiva in 1819 with an essay in *The Indicator* that begins by asserting the truth of the legend. Referring to Matthew Paris's description of Godiva mounting the horse, he observes, "What scene can be more touching to the imagination – beauty, modesty, feminine softness, a daring sympathy; an extravagance producing, by the nobleness of its object and the strange gentleness of its means, the grave and profound effect of the most reverend custom."[13]

Walter Savage Landor was prompted upon reading Hunt's essay to recall a Godiva procession in Coventry which had made a strong impression on him as a child, and it inspired his imaginary conversation between the newly married Godiva and Leofric while they ride on horseback into Coventry. After giving his rash promise (overheard by the bishop) Leofric muses on a strand of Godiva's hair that has come loose: "it mingleth now sweetly with the cloth of gold upon the saddle, running here and there, as if it had life and faculties and business, and were working thereupon some newer and cunninger device. O my beauteous Eve! there is a paradise about thee!"[14] Godiva privately contemplates the ride she will make the following day ("I shall be very pale") and hopes the people "will not crowd about me so."

Thirty-one years after his *Indicator* essay and eight years after Tennyson's poem, Hunt attempts "to do honour to the glorious Coventry heroine" by publishing his own poem on the subject. The long fourteeners on the printed page disguise the tetrameter-plus-trimeter rhythms of a ballad. In the following stanza, which describes the scene singled out by the 1819 essay as the emotional core of the story, Hunt uses every metrical trick he can muster:

The mass is said; the priest hath blessed the lady's pious will;
Then down the stair she comes undressed, but in a mantle still;
Her ladies are about her close, like mist about a star;
She speaks some little cheerful words, but knows not what they are;
The door is passed; the saddle pressed; her body feels the air;
Then down they let, from out its net, her locks of piteous hair.[15]

Each line is rhythmically segmented even more by internal rhyme (as with let/net), to which Hunt adds a network of supplemental rhymes and half-rhymes (said/blessed, passed/pressed, blessed/undressed/pressed). Even by the standards of poetry in 1850, it is a disastrous combination of elevated subject matter and sing-song balladeering. But Hunt at least manages to fulfill the wish expressed in his review to create a psychological portrait uncomplicated by the intrusion of contemporary reality. He presents his "Sweet saint" and "guiltless Eve" with a hagiographical reverence that directs more attention to the "feelings of the heroine's heart." But Hunt's idealization is not without attention to carnal details. What his essay calls the "feminine softness" of this scene has a graphically tactile referent in the poem: "the saddle pressed; her body feels the air." Once she has mounted the horse Godiva's maids somehow loosen her "piteous hair" – an instance of pathetic fallacy that neatly illustrates Hunt's Romantic conflation of the emotional and physical. Tennyson's more modern sensibilities were more likely to juxtapose (not conflate) the past and present, the ideal and real, or the emotional and physical.

For a number of reasons Hunt's poem has less in common with Tennyson's than it does with the folk ballads that had popularized Godiva's story since the sixteenth century. Most were anonymous. Visitors to the Coventry procession in the mid-nineteenth century encountered "minstrels who were singing of the lady in every street, and selling copies of each song for a half-penny each." For a penny they could purchase "The Coventry Garland," which printed a long ballad containing the following stanzas that one visitor considered "not without merit":[16]

And on that day, those ancient streets
With gloom were overspread,
And every house was clos'd as though
The inhabitants had fled;
Deserted and bare all seemed there,
Like a city of the dead.

> Each window clos'd, each door was barr'd:
>   And the people – where was they?
> The burthen'd vassals were all within:
>   They had hid themselves to pray
> That Heaven might speed the noble deed
>   Which rais'd their hopes that day.
>
> And forth she came, on a milk-white steed,
>   So beautiful and fair;
> No covering, save her innocence,
>   And her long and flowing hair.
> And thus, on her mission of mercy, she rode
>   Through the streets so gloomy and bare.
>
> And through those narrow and darksome streets
>   She pass'd like a vision of light,
> Or a pilgrim saint of charity
>   Performing an holy rite;
> But, Oh! such a pilgrim who hath seen,
>   Or a saint so fair and bright?
>
> And on she rode, 'mid solitude
>   And silence all around:
> A midnight stillness it seem'd to be,
>   Unbroken and profound:
> Save the echoing of her horse's tread,
>   That clank'd upon the ground.

Such ballads did more to popularize the legend than poems published for a more sophisticated readership, like those of Hunt or even Tennyson. Though it is hard to trace such ephemera (many of which have not survived), their readership extended well beyond the annual visitors to Coventry, but even on that occasion the potential market could be numbered in the tens of thousands. The ballads help explain how Godiva was received with an almost religious reverence in the nineteenth century. In the stanzas above, she is characterized by innocence and mercy, and as "a pilgrim saint of charity / Performing an holy rite." At the same time, ballads made Peeping Tom into a villain of unmitigated evil. In 1842, the same year that Tennyson's poem was published, a ballad by a local minister named H. W. Hawkes had "the immortal honour of being laid before her most gracious Majesty Queen Victoria."[17] The title page to the seventh edition claims that 17,000 copies had been sold. One can only guess what Victoria made of stanzas like the following:

Madam, he cried, pray stop your sighs –
  (He shook the very hall)
"If you'll ride naked through the town
  That shall quick clear them all."

.   .   .   .   .   .

When she told her astonish'd lord
  She would go through the task,
With the strict honour of his word
  All windows blinded fast.

That none should look into the street
  Upon sure pain of death,
Which was proclaim'd throughout the town –
  She started out of breath.

But then, before she mounted on
  Her palfry white and clear,
Her lovely tresses she let down
  To shade her bosom fair

.   .   .   .   .   .

O Tom how could'st thou act so rude
  To lady chaste and kind?
It proves thou wast of wicked heart,
  Likewise ungrateful mind.

But hadst thou known thy precious sight
  Would the sad forfeit be,
Thy rashness ne'er had prompted thee
  To peep at this lady.

Thou sure must have forgot thyself,
  Or duty to thy God
For he could see thee though shut up,
  And kill thee with a nod.

As wanting often proves the worth
  Of anything we crave
So thou went blinded all thy life,
  Unpity'd to the grave.

It would be only charitable to say the last two lines are "not without merit," and perhaps Victoria was generous enough to find the social platitudes reassuring. But aside from the immediate virtues of Hawkes's disastrous effort, balladeers like him were as responsible for the reverential reception of Godiva as the custodians of high culture.

Like Queen Victoria, women writers and activists found an appealing medieval heroine in Godiva, in part because they recognized the paradoxical nature of their own careers in the contraries that Tennyson and others had articulated. Anna Jameson fantasizes about Godiva's apotheosis (and her own) in her commonplace book: "If I were queen of England, I would have her painted in Fresco in my council chamber." Similarly, in explaining to Elizabeth Barrett her decision to speak publicly about her uterine tumor, Harriet Martineau writes, "I cannot tell you how the thought of *Godiva* has sustained and inspired me."[18] And Barrett Browning's *Aurora Leigh* (1857) may make subtle allusions to the legend in passages where suffering women loosen their clothing and release their hair to let it fall free.[19] What women of the middle class prized in the Godiva story was her willingness to risk public scandal for a higher moral good. Her movement proceeds from the home out into the public arena and back again with her virtue intact and society improved. And yet in spite of a man's authoritative control and the perils of public exposure, she projects a spellbinding erotic appeal.

Because the Godiva legend is so closely linked to the dynamics of male desire, its appropriation by women writers can seem problematic. For Harriet Martineau to speak of her uterine cancer in the context of Godiva's ride is to invoke the age-old equivalence of a woman's body with its reproductive and sexual roles in a patriarchal society. If the eroticism cannot be erased from the Godiva narrative, the question arises whether the writers had assimilated the dynamics of the male gaze to such an extent that they could see Godiva's self-display not merely as something shameful and dangerous but also as something positive: her erotic appeal allegorized as public fame. As authors and public speakers they craved public attention insofar as they wanted their books to sell and their voices to be heard. But because it might be self-defeating for women in the nineteenth century to admit openly to such an ambition, they found in Godiva's nakedness a model that combined both the anxiety *and* the desire for public exposure. After all, Godiva voluntarily if reluctantly undertakes the ride after Leofric imposes the conditions, and readers have been eager witnesses to the spectacle since the story's first appearance. Similarly, Victorian women writers placed themselves in the arena of public opinion despite conditions imposed by the patriarchal society. Their anxiety was less *that* they should be seen than *how* they would be seen. Their exposure had to be rescued by respectability. Here again the ambivalent dynamics of Tennyson's poem are helpful: of the two kinds of gaze, they shunned coarse voyeurism in favor of the guiltless readerly gaze. Whether the two could be so easily distinguished is another question.

The appeal of Godiva as a champion for the downtrodden becomes more problematic in Josephine Butler's *New Godiva*, a booklet that addresses the question of prostitution through a smoking-room dialogue between Cecil, recently returned from ten years in New Zealand, and his brother Victor. Cecil is shocked to learn that Victor's wife Mary has become involved in social work with prostitutes, and the bulk of the dialogue consists of Victor's arguments to justify society's obligation to its "victims," estimated to number 80,000 in London alone. Victor compares social workers like Mary to a latter-day Godiva,

> staking something dearer than life in the high emprise, stripping herself bare of the very vesture of her soul, rather than see the poor of her people become a prey, the rich given over to selfish indulgence and shortsighted cruelty. It is no hyperbolical phrase that I use when I say, "dearer than life."
>
> > "'You would not let your little finger ache
> > For such as *these*?' 'But I would die,' she said,"
>
> – the Godiva of old. And she *would* have died, probably would have preferred death to the grisly alternative which she accepted for the people's sake.
>
> From the new Godiva, too, a harder thing than the mere laying down of one's life has been required. From her, too, it has been exacted to place upon the altar *her reputation*, exposing herself to something worse than mere physical torture, to a species of misconception more exquisitely agonizing than the most ingenious refinement of bodily suffering.[20]

The short quotation from Tennyson's poem is repeated as an epigraph to the dialogue, but Godiva does not enter into the discussion until this passage, near the end of the pamphlet. Victor's rhetorical effort to deny hyperbole has just the opposite effect. Can any reader believe the literal claim that social workers would prefer physical torture to the loss of their reputation? But aside from the rhetorical excess, such "exquisitely agonizing" protests of self-sacrifice in the name of Godiva sidestep the eroticism in the legend. To make Godiva a martyr who places "upon the altar *her reputation*" is to make her a saint (which is what most narratives of the legend do), but saint and whore become a volatile combination as soon as the reader recalls that Godiva's reputation is based on the public display of her naked body. It would be as easy to select another set of details that makes Godiva a streetwalker or to turn her ride into a peep-show as it is to make her a de-eroticized, aestheticized martyr. But Butler's rhetoric and her invocation of Tennyson have a purpose.

As the leader of the Ladies' National Association in the 1870s and 1880s, Josephine Butler led a vigorous national campaign against the sexual hypocrisy of the Contagious Diseases Act, which prosecuted women presumed to be prostitutes, not the men who were their sexual partners, as carriers of venereal disease. The campaign involved both direct intervention with prostitutes on the street and formal public appearances before middle-class society and politicians. Although she worked for equality between the sexes, Butler and other women reformers of the time did not seek to overthrow the traditional domestic role for women. When she and other leaders of the LNA appeared in public, they felt deeply vulnerable in speaking about matters as openly sexual as prostitution. Nevertheless, Butler was a charismatic lecturer "who was adored by men and women alike."

> She was also sexually attractive to men. Meticulously coifed, dressed in the height of fashion, she held popular audiences spellbound with tales of instrumental rape, police brutality, and aristocratic corruption. The voyeuristic character of these spectacles was undoubtedly enhanced by the physical charms of the "lady" speaker.[21]

Because of her attractiveness, for Butler to raise an issue so directly related to sex was to risk implicating herself in it. But her physical presence reminded her audience that the difference between her and the class of women victimized by the Contagious Diseases Act was a matter of social definitions. The parallels with the Godiva legend go beyond the "voyeuristic character of these spectacles" and "the physical charms of the 'lady'" to the underlying principles motivating Butler. The legend becomes allegorical. Both Godiva and Butler are identified by their activism and their physical presence. The public exposure they undergo comes at a cost of emotional vulnerability. In both her rhetoric to middle-class audiences and her rescue work in working-class neighborhoods, Butler's journey takes her from her protected home into the marketplace of sex. The woman's body, even as it is eroticized by patriarchal authority, becomes a means to challenge that authority and change society.

There is another way that Queen Victoria's birthday gift to Albert reflects how the legend had become domesticated. The public spectacle at its heart, so prominently on display during the Coventry's Godiva processions, appealed to a radical change in the urban visual culture in England, which moved from classical models of optics to the emergence of what Jonathan Crary has called the "subjective observer."[22] It can be seen even in literary interpretations of the legend, such as Tennyson's poem, which shows a complex awareness of the dynamics of the viewer's position. The inherent spectacle of Godiva's ride and the object lesson that appealed to Victoria also made it a compelling subject for the fine arts. The viewer's gaze translates into perspective when artists manipulate it for aesthetic purposes. Landseer's painting *Lady Godiva's Prayer* (plate 4; discussed in chapter 4) is a useful reminder of the way the viewer's perspective is shaped by the different attitudes of the two women in the foreground. But Landseer's was only one of many engravings, paintings, and sculptures during the nineteenth century in which the more common of the two postures for Godiva is the downcast look of shame, quite often with the horse mimicking the gesture. Typical examples are William Behnes's *Lady Godiva*, which was displayed at the Great Exhibition in 1851, and John Thomas's larger-than-life statue from around 1860. A statue by C. B. Birch, which was displayed at the Royal Academy in 1884, uses another means to combine the looks of inspiration and shame.[23] Godiva stands on the mounting-stool with her back to the horse. She has just cast aside her cloak, which she clutches in one hand, and the other, palm up, rests on the horse's mane. Although the erect posture and distant gaze reveal no consciousness of her exposed body, the horse's head hangs down as if it (like Landseer's servingwoman) cannot bear to look.

Few artists attempt to use Godiva's hair to conceal her nakedness. Certainly complete concealment is harder to achieve in a work of art with any pretensions toward realism than it is in the imagination of a reader willing to suspend disbelief about hair's physical limits. No matter how Pre-Raphaelite in its profusion, the hair will always be inadequate. But most artists, beginning with Adam van Noort's sixteenth-century painting, prefer to use the hair less to hide than to highlight the body, as if it had the same function as drapery in classical nudes. Kenneth Clark's distinction between the idealized "nude" and the individuated "naked" body is useful to keep in mind.[24] The mere presence of functional garments, even if discarded on the ground, marks the body as naked, fixed in a particular time and place and erotically charged; the nude body, which might be accompanied by drapery (not clothing), inclines more toward pure form detached from any specific time and place. While the legend of Godiva is nothing if not the story of an individual having removed her clothes, artists have attempted to elevate the scene to one of classical timelessness. Thomas's or Behnes's sculptures, for example, offer a depersonalized nude on a horse with flowing hair and saddle blankets suggesting drapery. Thomas Woolner's half-life-size statue, exhibited at the Royal Academy in 1878, shows Godiva standing alone, easing down her robe, which has the effect of making her torso appear to be emerging from a base of classical drapery. Stephens (who disparaged Landseer's painting) described it as "the stately and beautiful statue in marble of Godiva disrobing, letting the last white garment of her sacrifice glide downwards to her feet," and rhapsodized that the far-away look on her face is so "gravely passionate and intensely pure – she thinks less of her nakedness than of her reward."[25]

While the Godiva story was part of a larger idealization of the Middle Ages in Victorian England, in most cases medievalism looked to the Arthurian legends for its themes and placed them in a setting of high Gothic style. But the Godiva legend offered artists, especially sculptors, the opportunity to adopt an Anglo-Saxon theme and to work in a style inspired by ancient Greece and Rome. It was an opportunity for medievalism and classicism to overlap. The Elgin marbles (to take the most famous example), removed from Athens by Thomas Bruce in 1806 and sold to the British government in 1816, formed part of a larger revival of interest in Greece and Rome as predecessors of Great Britain's enormous empire. While the early history of England provided few subjects that could be imagined alongside the Elgin marbles, what could be more appropriate than a nude and a horse?[26] Godiva offered a perfect subject for Victorian classicism, which favored female nudes over male, unlike the art of ancient Greece and Rome.

The Victorian impetus toward the classical could only be sustained by extracting the nude-and-horse subject from the larger context of the legend. But unlike Venus or a naiad (for example) Godiva could not escape her narrative, which necessarily gives every representation of her a local habitation and a name. Most artists deliberately compromised the classical ideal by showing Godiva's clothing flung aside (Birch) or a clothed companion (Landseer), but doing so enabled viewers to project the sturdy indigenous virtues of duty and self-sacrifice onto the eroticized subject. The idealized nude becomes the naked countess at the smallest sign of historical specificity, even by a gesture as slight as assigning it the name Godiva.

Any topic that attracts the kind of reverential hero-worshiping of Leigh Hunt, Edwin Landseer, and *The New Godiva* is ripe for parodic reversals. While the Victorian period saw some of the most ingenious send-ups, as early as the seventeenth century ways were found to exploit the comic potential in Lady Godiva's ride. The possible religious parody discussed in chapter 3 was an especially polarizing instance, yet the annual Coventry processions beginning in 1678 always incorporated an element of the carnivalesque in the day's celebration. It was a time to honor Lady Godiva, but not to worship her. But in highbrow literature such as Jago's "Edge Hill" of 1767 she had become an object lesson for an array of moral virtues and was thus a potential target for satirists. For instance, in 1784 a comic opera, *Peeping Tom of Coventry* by John O'Keeffe, was produced in London's Strand Theatre. The plot strays far from the familiar story of the legend, and Lady Godiva herself plays a surprisingly brief role, with no singing part.[27] Peeping Tom is the main character, and the rest of the cast is filled out with characters named after a hotchpotch collection from early English history – Maud, Emma, and Harold, as well as the earl of Mercia – and the mayor and mayoress of Coventry. The ride itself takes place offstage on Godiva's wedding day. Tom gets excited when he learns that Godiva will pass in front of his house, but the mayor orders him and all the citizens to clear the streets and shut up their houses. The mayor decides to "have a charming peek" for himself and, thinking that Tom has gone away, goes over to a window. Tom is already there, however, and after regaining his composure the mayor takes him to the earl for punishment. Tom uses his cleverness to escape hanging, and the earl fires the mayor and appoints Tom in his place. Something of the character of Tom can be glimpsed in the following lyrics from a song near the end of the opera:

> When I was a yonker and liv'd with my dad
> the neighbours all thought me a smart little lad
> My mammy she call'd me a white-headed boy
> because with the girls I lik'd to toy.[28]

Eleven years later the satirist John Wolcot (under the pen-name Peter Pindar) used the legend and the Coventry processions to lampoon the public appearances of George III, one of his favorite targets:

> By the sage counsel, possibly alone,
> Like Dame Godiva, George may travel on,
> When, lo, of curiosity a head,
> A peeping Tom, may from a window poke;
> Then let the bullet or the sabre's stroke
> Dismiss the saucy peeper to the dead.[29]

In 1821 a different kind of parody appeared in the *Etonian,* a journal
that had a run of only two years. Despite its brief run a long poem
called "Godiva – A Tale" by John Moultrie (under the pseudonym
G[eorge] M[ontgomery]) caught the attention of reviewers as different
in their tastes as William Gifford and William Wordsworth, who wrote
to an acquaintance that Moultrie was as "hopeful" as any of the young
writers; "if you should ever fall in with him tell him that he has pleased
me much." Gifford's approving notice in the *Quarterly Review* quotes
four and a half stanzas from "one of the serious passages, which strikes
us as singularly fine."[30] Two of the stanzas, which anticipate Leigh Hunt's
wish for a psychological portrait of Godiva, are given here:

LVII

The lady rose from prayer, with cheek o'erflush'd,
    And eyes all radiant with celestial fire,
The anguished beatings of her heart were hush'd,
    So calmly heavenward did her thoughts aspire.
A moment's pause – and then she deeply blush'd,
    As, trembling, she unclasp'd her rich attire,
And, shrinking from the sun-light, shone confest
The ripe and dazzling beauties of her breast.

LVIII

And when her white and radiant limbs lay bare,
    The fillet from her brow the dame unbound,
And let the traces of her raven hair
    Flow down in wavy lightness to the ground,
Till half they veil'd her limbs and bosom fair,
    In dark and shadowy beauty floating round,
As clouds, in the still firmament of June,
Shade the pale splendours of the midnight moon.

The description of Godiva disrobing in Tennyson's poem may owe something to this passage in Moultrie,[31] as may other details: Leofric's long
"flaxen locks," the clamoring mothers, his incomprehension at Godiva's
compassion ("How was it possible [she] . . . Could feel for wretches
quite in humble life?"). Moultrie's serious stanzas are offset by a greater
number indulging in an irreverent display of wit. It begins with twelve
stanzas that include digressions on youth, cricket, his muse, and Coventry's representative in Parliament. Leofric is a gluttonous churl, recently married to the chaste and beautiful Godiva, who responds to the
people's pleas for relief. Leofric is baffled by her compassion but thinks

he has hit upon a clever solution by his condition "That you ride naked through the public street." At this crucial moment the narrator intrudes with a characteristically self-conscious blend of sympathy, melodrama, and wit:

> XXXVI
> Godiva started – well indeed she might,
>   She almost doubted her own ears' veracity;
> My modest pen can scarce endure to write
>   A speech of such unparallel'd audacity.
> Leofric thought he had perplexed her quite,
>   And grinned immensely at his own sagacity;
> For which I hold him a consummate beast,
> Deserving of the pillory at least.

Only Godiva, it seems, escapes the satire. Elsewhere the reader is treated to digressions on the earl's diet, a geometry textbook, the scandal of the waltz, the annoyance of boring conversations, female boarding-schools, and the impropriety of women on horseback.

In 1851 another musical burlesque opened at the Strand Theatre in London: *Godiva; or, Ye Ladye of Coventrie and ye Exyle Fayrie*.[32] Peeping Tom is transformed into a reporter from the London newspaper *Busie Bee*, sent to Coventry to write a column on uprisings over wages and taxes. Godiva wants Leofric to give in to the citizens. He swears he'll be whipped before he agrees, so Godiva obliges and whips him with her riding crop; she then kicks him. Leofric tells her she must ride "au naturel" through the streets before he will grant her request. As Godiva prepares to disrobe, she gives a show-stopping Shakespearean parody that illustrates, among other things, the clever rhyming couplets used throughout:

> To be, or not to be, at his suggestion
> A Pose Plastique, is yet a doubtful question,
> To bare my arms against a Sea of troubles
> And by a pose to end them! Each day doubles
> The people's wrongs, the proud Earl's heavy tax;
> To help to ease them I would not be lax,
> But then to ride – riding, by some low scrub
> Perhaps to be seen! – Ah! bother – there's the rub
> The fear that still my courage may be less
> When I have shuffled off this mortal dress,
> Must give me pause.

The play also includes a send-up of the nursery rhyme "Ride a cock horse to Banbury Cross, To see a fine lady upon a fine horse" (which many people associate with the Godiva legend) and various other spoofs.

The satirists were not the only ones to poke holes in the legend's credibility. The nineteenth century in England saw the study of history mature into a "scientific" discipline. Professional scholars such as Edward A. Freeman, whose multi-volume *History of the Norman Conquest of England* is still a valuable resource, were supplanting earlier generations of amateur antiquarians. Freeman in particular had little patience for the Godiva legend. In a book of early English history that he wrote as "an experiment" for children, he recounts the familiar story before dismissing it as a worthless fabrication: "This is not one of the real old legends, which, though not true, are still for many reasons worth telling. It is a mere silly tale, which was not heard of till long after Leofric's time." But Freeman goes further and, not content with calling it a "mere silly tale," laments the harm it has done in distracting attention away from the valuable lessons of English history; finally, as if to avoid losing his temper altogether, he lightens the mood by poking fun at Frenchmen:

> And it really makes one almost angry to think how many people know such a foolish tale as this who never heard anything besides about the great Earl Leofric and his wife. And it is some comfort to think that, if there was a Peeping Tom of Coventry at this time, he must have been one of King Edward's Frenchmen, for Englishmen . . . did not use Scripture names.

One suspects that the ethnic chauvinism is not entirely in jest, and in fact the same sentiment appears in a footnote of his *History of the Norman Conquest*, the first volumes of which were appearing at about the same time as his *Old English History for Children*.[33] It is also clear that his ire was not directed at children or patriotic Englishmen, but at writers who promoted a "mere silly tale" as historical truth and who should have known better.

One such writer was the Reverend Charles Kingsley. Even Kingsley's staunchest admirers admit that he had less talent as a historian than as a moralist and fiction writer, but from 1860 to 1869 he held the post of Professor of Modern History at Cambridge University. His major work in this period was *Hereward the Wake, "Last of the English,"* a historical novel about a semi-legendary English resistance fighter against the new Norman masters of England after 1066.[34] By reading early chronicles with an uncritical eye and dramatically enlarging upon them, Kingsley makes Hereward a wayward son of Lady Godiva, and his stubborn refusal to submit to the Norman yoke shows that the native English still had some fight left in them. Kingsley's university lectures, which formed the basis of the book, took up the legend as well. Thirty years later one of his students fondly referred to Kingsley as "that most poetic teacher," whose lectures fired "the spirit of romance and chivalry" with such tales as Hereward the Wake.[35] While Kingsley's account emphasizes Godiva's piety and generosity to monasteries to the point that the monks have an inordinate hold over her, he alludes to "a far nobler deed" in Coventry that has made her name known to all. The chance to tie Hereward's legendary fame to Lady Godiva's was too tempting for Kingsley to pass up (though historically suspect), but the obliqueness of the reference to her ride suggests an awareness that its veracity was suspect. An indirect allusion in a work of historical fiction allowed him to have it both ways.

In the ten years during which Kingsley used his professorship to preach a moralistic view of the past, Freeman labored as a freelance historian and gradually established his reputation by means of a constant stream of reviews, articles, and books. Even Kingsley admits Freeman's abilities as a historian by referring to "a little paper controversy" on the life of Godwine, in which Freeman "has proved himself to have been in the right, while I was in the wrong."[36] After many years Freeman's labors were rewarded by his appointment as Professor of Modern History at Oxford in 1884, but in the 1860s he would have been more than a little annoyed to see a post as distinguished as a professorship at Cambridge occupied by a man with little understanding of the emerging modern discipline of history and who did nothing to correct the popular reception of the "mere silly tale" of Godiva's ride.

While Kingsley's efforts aroused the ire of Freeman, their different approaches illustrate how easy it is for the Godiva legend to shift from the sublime to the ridiculous. What was true among the educated elite was unambiguously reflected in popular culture. In an 1895 exhibit of "Living Pictures" at London's Palace Theatre, Lady Godiva found herself included among naiads, peris, and mountain sprites, all represented in various states of undress. It was clearly a prurient spectacle masquerading as high art. The exhibit prompted denunciations by the National Vigilance Association, on whose behalf William Alexander Coote denounced the displays as "the ideal form of indecency," and "shameful productions, deserving the condemnation of all right-thinking people." Coote's self-righteousness inspired George Bernard Shaw, who had re-

cently begun work as drama critic for the *Saturday Review*, to go immediately to the Palace Theatre,

> not because I wanted to wallow in indecency – no man in his senses
> would go to a public theatre with that object even in the most abandoned
> condition of public taste, privacy being a necessary condition of thor-
> ough-going indecency – but because, as a critic, I at once perceived that
> Mr. Coote had placed before the public an issue of considerable moment:
> namely, whether Mr. Coote's opinion is worth anything or not. For Mr.
> Coote is a person of real importance.

He endured the entire production of sixteen "Living Pictures," all of
which were played by very pretty women "except perhaps Lady Godiva."
It is only too obvious to the experienced eye of a critic, he assures his
audience, that what was offered as exposed flesh was really spun silk.
And the actresses' state of modesty and cleanliness turned out to be no
worse than that of some of the elaborately dressed women in the audience. He commends them as an aesthetic and hygienic model for young
women. "In short, the living pictures are not only works of art: they are
excellent practical sermons; and I urge every father of a family who
cannot afford to send his daughters the round of the picture galleries in
the Haymarket and Bond Street, to take them all (with their brothers)
to the Palace Theatre." Setting aside satire for a direct assault, he concludes that Mr. Coote is "in artistic matters a most intensely stupid man,
and on sexual questions something of a monomaniac."[37]

During the whole of this period, as a kind of backdrop to the literature and to the exhibitions in London and elsewhere, the Coventry
procession was held on a regular basis, and as the main event during a
festive occasion it could not take itself too seriously. Local wits knew
how to whet the anticipation of visitors by goading them with whis-
pered confidences that "this year" the actress would "really" be naked.
And the Peeping Tom statue, with its grotesque facial expression, has
always cut a ridiculous figure. Throughout England the carnivalesque
and satirical treatments of Godiva reached their peak in the nineteenth
century, when the reception of the legend was at its most reverential.
When the twentieth and twenty-first centuries have bothered to take
the legend seriously, it has been as a cultural myth rather than history,
and so it provides less of an occasion for social satire. Just how the
legend progressed through the twentieth century is a story in its own
right.

Chapter 6

Godiva Displayed

The beautiful legend of Lady Godiva tells how all the town's inhabitants hid behind their shuttered windows, so as to make easier the lady's task of riding naked through the streets in broad daylight, and how the only man who peeped through the shutters at her revealed loveliness was punished by going blind.

(Dr. Freud)

Today Lady Godiva brings to mind a shameful picture – a big blond nude trotting around the town on a horse. In the background of this picture, there is always Peeping Tom, an illicit snooper with questionable intentions.

(Dr. Seuss)

The widespread familiarity with the Godiva legend in the nineteenth century made it so commonplace that two of the most famous doctors of the twentieth century could drop the allusions quoted above, confident that their readers would fill in the details. In fact, the dismissiveness of Dr. Seuss's summary – "a big blond nude trotting around the town" – suggests an *over*familiarity, as if the story has grown tedious from being heard too many times. Despite their contrary verdicts ("beautiful" versus "shameful") and the differences in tone between the clinical seriousness of one and the mischievousness of the other, it is remarkable how much the two summaries have in common. Both fail to mention any motivation for the ride: no Leofric, taxation, or even Coventry. Godiva merely rides naked through the streets of a town, observed by a solitary voyeur. Both assume a moral contrast between Godiva's public nakedness and Tom's "illicit" voyeurism that deserves to be "punished." And each emphasizes the role of sight in the mental "picture" they draw.

After summarizing the traditional legend in the passage above, Dr. Seuss rewrites it as the story of seven Godiva sisters ("history's barest family"), who must complete a quest to marry Peeping Tom, Peeping Dick, Peeping Harry, and the other four Peeping brothers (plate 5). The action takes place in 1066, just after Lord Godiva, earl of Coventry, is thrown from his horse and killed on the way to the battle of Hastings.

> Seven hands clasped over Lord Godiva's remains. Seven tongues spoke. Seven pledges were uttered.
> "I swear," swore each, "that I shall not wed until I have brought to the light of this world some new and worthy Horse Truth, of benefit to man."
> It was an oath of heroic proportions.[1]

The plot follows the adventures of each of the seven sisters as they search for a Horse Truth (for example, never look a gift horse in the mouth). They are naked because, as Lord Godiva is proud to observe, they have sworn off clothing as an unnecessary frivolity. (Lord Godiva and the seven Peeping brothers, however, are fully clothed.) Lady Godiva, it turns out, is conspicuously absent. She is not even mentioned, although "Godiva" is now the family name and her nakedness has been assumed by the sisters. The reader can infer that Lady Godiva is the missing wife and mother, who must have died already because the seven daughters are left alone to seek out their horse truths.

It seems fitting, in light of the children's books for which Dr. Seuss later became famous, that when he recast the legend for adult readers he gave it an absurdly improbable plot. Before 1957, when he finally hit upon his formula for commercial success with *The Cat in the Hat*, Theodore Seuss Geisel struggled for decades as a cartoonist and author. *The Seven Lady Godivas* (1939) was one of his earliest independent efforts, which he described to his publisher as "an adult book with naked ladies." It was a commercial failure, and it failed again in 1987 when it was "Reissued by Multitudinous Demand" (and as a favor by his publisher to Geisel). Apparently the reading public is not yet ready for a book of exaggerated breasts and buttocks caricatured in Dr. Seuss's distinctive style.[2]

Dr. Freud's invocation of Lady Godiva comes in a short discussion of psychically induced disorders of sight, and in particular the talion punishment (i.e. equal retribution) of scopophiliacs. He likens the psychical process to an accusing voice within the voyeur that says, "Because you sought to misuse your organ of sight for evil sensual pleasures, it is fitting that you should not see anything at all any more." He goes on to single out "the beautiful legend of Lady Godiva" as a typical example of talion punishment and adds that other myths can be explained similarly by reference to neurotic illness.[3] It should be noted that the talion punishment is not equal to the transgression in the strict "eye for an eye" sense, but is based on a symbolic equivalence between the loss of eyesight and its repeated misuse. As a well-attested substitute for castration, blindness may have added to the legend's appropriateness for Freud's purposes (though he does not mention it in this context). In other myths of voyeurs, such as Actaeon and Diana or Susannah and the Elders, the punishment is death. Thus Freud's interest in the "beautiful legend" seems to be directed more to Peeping Tom than to Godiva.

In a paper written a few years later Freud again raises the subject of scopophilia, but this time along with its opposite, exhibitionism, which together constitute a pair of complementary instincts "whose respective aim is to look and to display oneself."[4] The pairing arises as two stages in the same process, which begins with the autoerotic activity of a child looking at its own sexual organ. The active (looking) and passive (being looked at) components of this preliminary stage are the source of the later stages of looking at someone else's body (scopophilia) and putting one's body on display (exhibitionism). It would be disingenuous to fault Freud for failing to employ the Godiva legend as an apt illustration of the scopophilic instinct, but it corresponds remarkably well to the relations he analyzes. Ever since the introduction of the voyeur in the seventeenth century, the legend has set Godiva as exhibitionist and Tom as scopophiliac in a complementary relation to one another. Not all versions of the legend take advantage of the opportunity, but many of the more interesting ones do so by inviting one kind of identification with Godiva as hero and displacing another with Tom as scapegoat. The first stage in Freud's analysis of the scopophilic instinct – the self-gazing, autoerotic stage – is not represented except perhaps in some works of art where Godiva seems to survey her own body, as with John Collier's painting from around 1898 (plate 7).

There remain a few points to be made about the ways that Dr. Seuss and Dr. Freud appropriate the Godiva legend. Each version typifies one of the two strands in the twentieth-century reception of the story, which derive separately from the largely reverential Victorian reception. One strand features a playfully erotic Godiva, in which shame and guilt have been reduced to a kind of naughtiness. The other invokes the legend as a means to explore the dynamics of the voyeuristic gaze, along with a

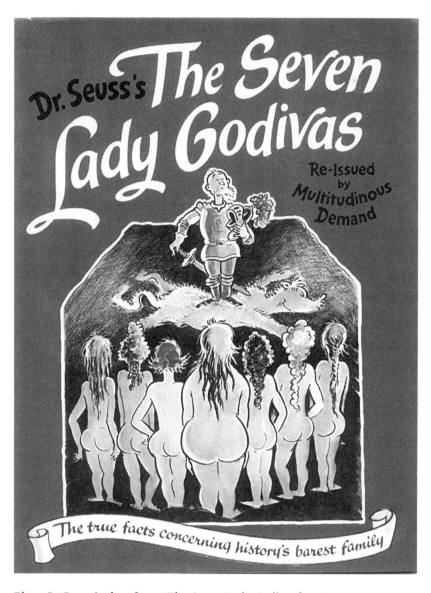

Plate 5   Dust-jacket from *The Seven Lady Godivas* by Dr. Seuss, TM &
copyright © by Dr. Seuss Enterprises, L.P. 1939, renewed 1967. Used
by permission of Random House Inc. and International Creative Man-
agement, Inc.

cluster of related ethical and psychological issues that have been raised before and after Freud. Whether trivial or weighty, the legend in the twentieth century circulated far outside of England so that it almost passes without comment that a Viennese psychoanalyst and a New York humorist find a story from medieval Coventry convenient for very different purposes.

In my informal surveys over the years nearly everyone I have questioned about Godiva recognizes the name. Many have known it for so long that they cannot recall when they first heard of it. The younger the informants and the farther they are from Coventry, the less likely they are to know the details of the older legend. About half can place Godiva in England, a few even specify Coventry, but almost no one associates her with pre-Conquest England because (as the thinking goes) it is not decadent enough for such a sexy story. Relatively few recognize Leofric, the taxation, or the condition for the ride, and many are surprised to learn that Peeping Tom is a part of the legend, just as many are surprised to learn that the legend is a fiction attached to the name of a historical woman. Many who recall an association with taxation think of the ride as a kind of tax protest. It seems that Godiva is becoming identified (as one of my students put it) as "a naked woman with long hair riding on a horse" who lived at some time in the past when people used horses to get around. Of course it would be unwise to push such anecdotal impressions too far, but one result is clear: the legend is losing its narrative. The image that remains is provocative, but it lacks the richness of detail that the story had from its beginning with the thirteenth-century chroniclers.

One of the responses that Godiva provokes, at least in my inquiries on the subject, is a smile of recognition, as if the image has pleasant or humorous associations. Her nakedness has a fairy-tale quality of innocence, or if not innocence at most an easily forgiven transgression. She seems to be admired for her sexiness, of course, but even more for her audacity in displaying her physical beauty to the public's admiring gaze. The smile of recognition seems to say that Godiva has got something that everyone desires: who would not want to be beautiful, desired, and unburdened by guilt and shame? Her image does not come charged with the moral force of the narratives that circulated in the nineteenth century and earlier. She is not the Godiva who made impassioned pleas to her husband, who was coerced into a choice between the citizens' well-being and her own modesty, and who made the ride in spite of the shame it threatened. The story also comes uncomplicated by the guilt of voyeurism. Peeping Tom has gone off on a career of his own. Godiva rides. Everyone gazes. And everyone winks. The smile-provoking associations and the simplicity of the image make it an easy target for one-liners like W. C. Fields's "Lady Godiva put everything she had on a horse."

In my casual inquiries I could not detect any differences in the way women and men view the legend, although I am sure such differences exist. Given the history of the legend as a vehicle for male erotic fantasies, the similarities of response might be surprising, but an image or brief anecdote might be more malleable or carry less ideological freight than a full-fledged narrative. Both men and women smile in recognition at the name; both know the same few details; both learned of it in childhood. I imagine that both are just as likely to laugh at the one-liners. Much depends, of course, on how the legend is remembered, and if vague memories of the plot are involved, the moral motivation for Lady Godiva's ride can shift to align itself with more contemporary heroic virtues. For example, the theme song to an American television sitcom in the early 1970s, *Maude*, elevates Lady Godiva to a tongue-in-cheek pantheon of women who changed history, including Joan of Arc, Isadora Duncan, and Betsy Ross: "Lady Godiva was a freedom rider, / She didn't care if the whole world looked. / Joan of Arc with the Lord to guide her, / She was a sister who really cooked."[5] *Maude*, as Norman Lear's quasi-feminist sequel to *All in the Family*, used humor to tackle controversial topics such as abortion (within a few years after Roe v. Wade). The lighthearted lyrics make it clear that Lady Godiva has been reinterpreted as an early champion of women's liberation from male oppression.

In surveys of my students a surprising number gave Belgium as the location for the story, which puzzled me until I recalled Godiva chocolates. Perhaps they were having a little joke at their teacher's expense (Hershey, Pennsylvania also appeared), but it could also be a shrewd guess that a Belgian chocolatier might make use of a local legend. Since its founding in 1926 Godiva Chocolatier has built an international reputation for premium chocolates. The company's reputation has been so positive, in fact, that in recent years the Campbell Soup Company, a conglomerate based in New Jersey, acquired Godiva Chocolatier and began an ambitious marketing campaign in the United States, Europe, Japan, and other industrialized countries. In the United States alone there are more than 260 Godiva boutiques and over 1,000 outlets in department stores and other upscale locations. The product is advertised in upper-tier magazines such as *Elle, Bon Appétit, Food and Wine,* and *Gourmet,* where the efforts have been so successful that the product's image is very possibly the most recognizable representation of Lady Godiva today (plate 6). It shows her on an extravagantly caparisoned horse with hair and mane swirling in elegant but stylized patterns, almost making horse and rider visually inseparable. Her head is erect and her gaze straight ahead, as if her exposed state is a matter of no concern or even a matter of pride, quite unlike the portrayals in Victorian art. In the 1990s the company's advertising image, with white outlines against a dark background, gave way to a "shadow" campaign with light outlines against a gold background in order to present "a more approachable, warmer, more friendly image."[6]

GODIVA
Chocolatier

Plate 6 Godiva Chocolatier

Perhaps the company's marketing efforts do not deserve such close attention, but the point it makes better than any survey is that the popular image of Godiva appeals as much to women as men, if not more. Godiva Chocolatier's customer base is primarily young to middle-aged women with a college education and a healthy income; the readership of gourmet food magazines such as *Bon Appétit* is, again, primarily educated women with disposable income. So it is vital that the advertising image of Godiva not only be approachable and warm, but that the nakedness must be as inoffensive as canned soup. While the chocolate Godiva cannot seem to be suffering from moral conflicts or shame, the appeal is heightened if a minor transgression is associated with the image because everyone knows that forbidden pleasures are the most enjoyable. Without the larger narrative to explain that she was coerced into riding naked, the responsibility for her action falls on Godiva herself. She seems to be unclothed by her own volition, nor does she seem to be suffering from the shame that one usually associates with being found naked in public, as in the earlier versions of the legend. The consumers targeted by the advertising campaign seem to admire Godiva's audacity in the display of her body, and dismiss any residual shame as a trivial breach of social etiquette. The genius of the marketing image is the way it uses guilt to augment desire: when presented with a box of chocolates, many people will hesitate at the prospect of calories and saturated fat ("Oh, I really shouldn't") only to give in and indulge ("Well, just one"). It is an easily forgiven, repeatedly forgiven peccadillo. The company packages a diet-busting temptation within an image of a slender, idealized body, for which the admiring gaze is eager to forgive any guilt. The company also revives (unwittingly, it seems) the older context of the ride through the marketplace of Coventry by promoting gold-foiled chocolate covered medallions, which are designed to look like coins inscribed with Godiva's image. Considered as simulacra of money, they are tokens of exchange intended to circulate through the marketplace without passing into any individual's possession (just as the legendary Godiva rode through unseen and therefore unpossessed, and returned home to her husband); but as chocolate confections they also become tokens of conspicuous consumption, as if peeling away the foil and eating them is a destruction of wealth – a costly privilege reserved for those with discerning taste.

The example from Godiva Chocolatier shows that even when the older narrative has been reduced to an image, it still conveys significant cultural messages. Its newer iconic function seems to provide a space for the free play of fantasies unburdened by social judgments on such things as illicit desire, body image, and privacy. In this atmosphere it is inevitable that the free play would result in humorous spoofs such as Dr. Seuss's *Seven Lady Godivas*. Parodic reversals have a long history, though before the twentieth century they responded to the reverence with which the legend was popularly received. In the twentieth century the light-hearted, unselfconscious image is what most people associate with Godiva, not the woman who in Tennyson's words "underwent, and overcame." Thus the comedy depends less on manipulating elements from the traditional plot and moves more directly to the broader social judgments that stand behind it. Godiva becomes the vehicle for the satire, not part of the target. The uses to which the legend is put tend to stay away from enlightened edification. They tend instead to veer toward the trivial. For example, the recently rediscovered manuscript by Margaret Mitchell, *Oh! Lady Godiva!*, written in 1926, takes up the traditional legend only incidentally. The plot involves a search to find a woman to play the role of Lady Godiva in an amateur play, but every available candidate in the town has bobbed her hair, after the fashion of the day.[7]

A number of pop songs have drawn their themes from Godiva or Peeping Tom. The biggest commercial success of these is the hit by Peter and Gordon, which made it to number 6 on the American pop charts in late 1966.[8] The lyrics begin:

> Seventeen, a beauty queen,
> she made her ride that caused a scene
> in the town.
> Her long blonde hair
> hanging down around her knees
> all the cats who dig striptease
> prayin' for a little breeze.
> Her long blonde hair,
> falling down across her arms
> hidin' all the lady's charms:
> Lady Godiva.

She turns down a Hollywood contract ("that was Lady G's mistake"), and ends up destitute, forced to cut her long blonde hair for cash. Peter and Gordon's song is another *reductio ad absurdum* of the legend, but Godiva as very young and blonde merely continues a trend that can be seen as early as Walter Savage Landor in the early nineteenth century. What is more characteristic of the twentieth century is the lack of motivation for her nakedness: no heroism or coercion. Her ride is presented as merely the occasion to display her naked body. In this regard it helps to remember that when Peter and Gordon wrote the song in the mid-1960s the Godiva processions in Coventry were still a recent memory. But after the procession of 1962 there was a long hiatus which coincided with the rise of the women's movement in England and elsewhere.

Blonde is the color of Godiva's hair in Peter and Gordon's lyrics as well as in almost all twentieth-century versions of the story, not merely because it makes her "fair," but because popular culture considers it sexy ("blondes have more fun") and perhaps because in some cases Godiva is seen to be confused or thoughtless ("the dumb blonde"). While the twentieth century preferred blondes, in the nineteenth century and earlier Godiva was as likely to be auburn-haired, or her hair color was not specified at all, as in Tennyson's poem. Moultrie's poem of 1822 gives Godiva "raven" hair (as opposed to Leofric's long "flaxen locks"), while in Landor's 1829 "Conversation" she has golden hair. Similarly, the women who impersonate Godiva in the Coventry processions have been hired, it seems, without regard to hair color. Painters too, before the twentieth century, did not favor one color over another. While light hair might reinforce the image of Godiva as fair, darker hair allowed artists like Collier to highlight the aesthetic contrast between the concealing hair and the whiteness of the skin revealed beneath.

Even more serious purposes to which the legend is put in the twentieth century can have something absurd about them. The lyrics for *Maude* (quoted above in this chapter), for example, construe Godiva as a "freedom rider," which seems to derive from a relatively recent interpretation of her ride as a protest. This new role was illustrated in 1996 by a protester who "threw off her coat and stood naked in front of 1,000 worshippers in Coventry Cathedral . . . interrupting a service marking the centenary of Britain's car industry."[9] Her body painted with slogans, she told the congregation that she was there to decry the 17 million people killed by the automobile. Hers was not the only protest, and the protests were not the only unusual events during the service, which included two automobiles driven up to the altar. When asked about the demonstrations after the service, the bishop of Coventry said, "It is a pity. I am only sorry that they couldn't have done it with a little more dignity and restraint."

Although the light-hearted and trivialized image of Godiva is now the most widely circulated representation, a more serious strand of the legend in its longer narrative form persisted in the first decades of the twentieth century. In the German-speaking world, for example, the Godiva legend underwent a surge of popularity at the turn of the century which helps account for the brevity of Freud's allusion. While it was well known in the Low Countries, and versions in Spanish, Russian, and French appeared in the first decades of the twentieth century, no other part of mainland Europe could match the German-speaking countries in their artistic and literary fascination with Godiva.[10] Between 1906 and 1907 alone there appeared two short stories, a ballad, and a bronze statue. Well before 1900, Tennyson's poem had gained a wide circulation with the help of two translations (in 1846 and 1867), and the legend could also be found in a translation of Dugdale's *Antiquities of Warwickshire* and in other summaries of English medieval history. The early Latin chronicles were also accessible to anyone with formal education. Between 1911 and 1919 (the years immediately following Freud's essay), there appeared no fewer than four plays on the subject, as well as another bronze statue, which was exhibited in Vienna in 1911–12.[11] All of these works sustained the reverential yet erotic Victorian interpretation of the legend. Thus when Freud mentioned "the beautiful legend of Lady Godiva" in his contribution to a Festschrift in honor of an old friend, he did not bother to summarize it or explain its relevance to talion punishment. He could expect his audience to be well acquainted with Godiva's heroic suffering, her beauty, her position as the erotic object of the voyeur's gaze, and what the voyeur did to deserve punishment.

How has the legend come to split into two separate strands: one involving the superficially erotic Godiva as she is popularly known and the other concerned with the transgressive gaze that deserves punishment? Perhaps more than any other version Tennyson's poem of 1842 was responsible for articulating the binary opposites in the older legend, which made it possible for later interpretations to select out elements that eventually comprised separate narratives. In John Collier's painting (plate 7) Godiva's youthful, slender body and her posture begin an interpretive shift away from the idealized object-lessons of most Victorian artists. She rides astride the horse, not side-saddle, which is at once more historically accurate (side-saddle was introduced by Anne of Bohemia in the fourteenth century), and allows Godiva to lean back and look down at the same time. Her posture is neither one of otherworldly inspiration like Landseer's Godiva nor one of shame; indeed she gives no visible sign of awareness that she is being watched. Instead the relaxed muscles (the leg and foot especially) make her seem less vulnerable and more meditative, even coy, in her self-absorbed gaze. The horse by contrast is alert and full of animal vigor, with no apparent mirroring of Godiva's emotional state, although it suggests sexual energy. Collier's composition is a transitional step toward the twentieth century's bifurcation of the legend into two images: Lady Godiva on display, and Peeping Tom as voyeur. In popular and high culture the two have increasingly come to be seen as independent images.

Plate 7 John Collier, *Lady Godiva*, ca. 1898

As just one example, the opening lines of W. H. Auden's "Cave of Nakedness" (1959), which demystifies the ordinary task of undressing for bed in comparison with romanticized conventions, invokes "Peeping Tom" as simply a name for a common voyeur:

> Don Juan needs no bed, being far too impatient to undress,
> nor do Tristan and Isolda, much too in love to care
>   for so mundane a matter, but unmythical
> mortals require one, and prefer to take their clothes off,
>   if only to sleep. That is why bedroom farces
> must be incredible to be funny, why Peeping Toms
>   are never praised, like novelists or bird-watchers
> for their keenness of observation: where there's a bed,
>   be it a nun's restricted cot or an Emperor's
> baldachined and nightly-redamselled couch, there are no
>   effable data.[12]

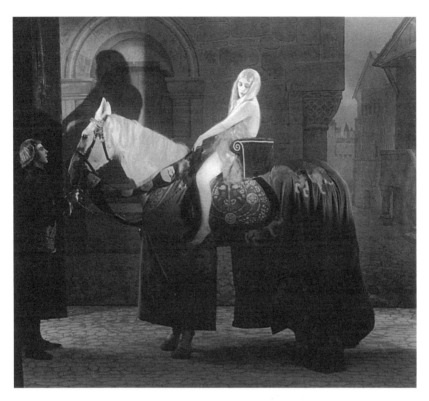

Plate 8 Lil Dagover in a *tableau vivant* of Collier's *Lady Godiva*, from
His English Wife (Hans Engelska Fru), 1927

What is "incredible" about bedroom farces is the way they reverse the
usual clumsiness of moving around in bed and the ease of spotting strangers even in the dark, so that identity becomes obscured and movement is effortless. In a medieval fabliau, for example, a clever clerk
might use a trick to leap into bed with a young wife, who then fails to
recognize the impostor until too late. Part of the humor is recognizing
that sex performed so heedlessly and efficiently with a stranger in the
dark (no fumbling, no groping) does not happen in real life. Conversely,
the often awkward physical movements of "unmythical mortals" undressing and getting into bed make the tasks of back-alley Peeping Toms
easier. What seems so unromantic from a literary point of view plays
into the hands of the voyeur, for whom the inevitable missteps only

Plate 9 Maureen O'Hara in the title role of *Lady Godiva*, 1955

prolong the pleasure, and which are so obvious that he deserves no praise for his "keenness of observation." As the great human leveller the bed fails to provide "effable data," not in the sense that what is given ("data") is ineffably sublime, but that what it gives is so common that it is beneath the attention of poets and lovers. (In this sense "effable" is the opposite of "ineffable"; but it also has an archaic meaning of "what can be lawfully expressed.") Of course the point of the poem is to make something of such unpromising material.

Plate 10 Jules J. Lefebvre, *Lady Godiva*, 1890

Even when writers invoke a more complete version of the older legend, they tend to highlight the aggressiveness of the voyeuristic gaze at
the expense of Godiva's traditional heroism. Alberto Moravia, for example, rewrites the legend as a short story told from the point of view
of a woman whose husband fantasizes about her as Lady Godiva.[13] He
repeatedly entreats her to indulge his fantasy by riding on horseback
with her hair loosened around her naked body. She is repulsed by the
notion, but she finally succumbs to a bribe to do it, just once. The husband gets his way by preying on her love of horses and promising to
buy her an expensive stallion she craves. She performs the ride late one
night. Spellbound by her performance, the man fails to notice the horse

circling closer and closer to him, until it willfully rears up and kicks him in the head, killing him. In the husband's character Leofric and Peeping Tom have merged and receive the punishment originally reserved for the voyeur. Because the punishment is administered by a non-human agency, it carries with it a sense of transcendent justice, as in the older legend. Moravia's short story helps illustrate another peculiarity about the Godiva legend. Prose fiction is one of the least used genres for the story. It seems to lend itself better to other genres and forms of expression (ballads, lyric poetry, processions, painting, sculpture, film). The difficulty cannot be with prose itself, because the early chronicle entries were Latin and English prose. It is more likely that more concrete forms of expression, especially processions and the plastic arts, bring the dynamics of the voyeuristic gaze into the foreground. Moreover, because the story is so well known and the plot so uncomplicated the fiction writers who have taken it up change it a great deal.

For example, Raoul Faure's 1948 novel *Lady Godiva and Master Tom* rewrites the legend as if it were *Madame Bovary* set in Anglo-Saxon England. Godiva becomes capricious, voluptuous, and treacherous, in part because she is bored and unthinking: "Her back to the stained-glass window, Lady Godiva was lost in thought, or rather she imagined she was lost in thought; actually her mind was empty. Most of the time she realized that her mind was empty, as if her total body were devoid of purpose; she felt slack, springless, unhappy. She did not know what to do with herself."[14] Godiva rides naked not to relieve citizens of taxes – that is a pretext her husband and his scheming Jewish adviser Ezra devise – but out of a vague impulse to degrade herself publicly and to make a beautiful spectacle of herself. The ride itself is described from the point of view of Godiva's excited imagination and heightened awareness of her body. Ennui gives way to a feeling of sexual empowerment that is so strong it even overcomes her shame:

> She was strong limbed and strong bodied and her heart was high. She would lean over the rim of the world and call whatever lover took her fancy and the wretch would run to her. She was a big fruit full of pulp and juice and of seeds that would lodge between the teeth. She was a world humped with hills and dales and murmurous heather; the sap of the earth came up directly into her and she received its thrust on the hinges of her hips; the wind and the light took root in her and spread into tortuous channels. She was a big, round loaf of bread rising under the leaven, a haystack smoking in the hard sun. Men ran away whimpering before her anger and her desire like fieldmice before the reaping hooks and they lay

quivering in the last ridge of barley. Her eyes glowed like live coals, her tongue tasted of hydromel and burned like acid, and her strength rose in her arms like two great bubbles. She would take men by the scruff of their necks and flatten them against the mountains of her body and she would keep them there until their marrow and the juice of their muscles drained and they sank away from her, their empty husks rattling.[15]

Like the images in a Hieronymus Bosch painting, the language combines folksy earth-lore and apocalyptic doom to convey Faure's idea of a fertility goddess's primal sexuality. But the release of heightened self-consciousness seems to end with the ride, and Godiva reverts to predictable behavior that makes her vulnerable to the plots of men around her. Peeping Tom is a good-hearted young tailor who fails to hear the decree to keep shut up indoors and unwittingly looks at Lady Godiva. When he is seized and brought before her, Godiva is both enraged and smitten by love. At first she demands that he be blinded, but she soon relents and becomes his lover. Together they become conspirators in a Norman plot to murder her husband Leofric and arrange a political marriage between Godiva and a Norman prince. The novel is, in the end, an unsuccessful (not to mention unhistorical) retelling of the legend, but John Steinbeck, who called it "a blistering study of a woman," was impressed enough to use Faure's Lady Godiva as an inspiration for Cathy Ames in *East of Eden*.[16]

Lewis Sowden takes a similarly inventive approach to the traditional story in his *Lady of Coventry*. Much of the plot revolves around an affair between "Leveric of Mercia" and a young peasant girl, who may or may not be his daughter by an earlier peasant lover. Godiva spends her time in study, in prayer, and in caring for the wretched inhabitants of Coventry, who are oppressed by Leveric's heavy taxation. Under the spiritual influence of the monks, she is pious and reserved, but on one occasion she gives herself to a handsome young monk named Alwyn, who is smitten by her beauty. In a subplot, a delegation of Coventry's merchants meets to convince Leveric to lift all taxes except for one on horses. At a crucial moment, when his lover is dying, his wife's perfidy is revealed to him, and the merchants are clamoring for tax relief, Leveric hits upon the plan for her naked ride. He does it to punish his wife; she does it to expiate guilt. The grateful citizens do their part to obey Leveric's mandate and remain shut up indoors.

It was a warm but dullish day. There was a gentle stir in the air which Godiva felt caressing her shoulders. Her breasts rose and fell with her

quick breathing. She sat her horse firm and upright, both hands on the reins. In the open light of day her skin was pale like mist. With the movement of the horse, her hair slipped round to her sides. . . .
Was this atonement, she asked herself. Was it as easy as this?[17]

During the ride her mind, in a dreamlike state of bewilderment, is filled with similar questions of motivation and consequence. Afterwards, Alwyn boasts publicly in the marketplace that he looked upon her as she rode. When he is brought to Leveric for questioning, Alwyn readily admits to the deed, but it becomes clear that he does so because he is racked by guilt and desires to be punished. After Leveric refuses to give him that satisfaction and sends him away, Alwyn blinds himself. In the end the citizens are relieved of the heavy burden of tax, and Leveric and Godiva are reconciled.

In a 1968 play that describes itself as "beyond the absurd," Ronald Tavel foregrounds the themes of voyeurism and sex without any of the ennobling qualities of the older legend. Besides Godiva, Tom, and Leofric the cast includes the sheriff Thorold, a chorus of singing nuns and a transvestite mother superior named Superviva. The plot is little more than a delayed anticipation of the naked ride, which all the characters assume will end the play. Throughout there are references to the legend in formally academic language. For example, near the beginning Godiva, a whore dressed like a Gibson Girl, introduces herself:

> GODIVA. Who am I? I am Godiva. Lady Godiva.
> SUPERVIVA. Lady, huh? Never knew the hooer who didn't claim she was a lady.
> GODIVA. But I *am* a lady. I am Lady Godiva. Don't you believe me?
> SUPERVIVA. Certainly not! I never believed that horse maneuver about Lady Godiva. So far as I'm concerned, it's all just a symbolic tale. Godiva divested herself symbolically: i.e., she stripped herself of her superfluous jewels in order to pay the levied tax.
> GODIVA. You'll find my tail (*swishing her rump*) is not all that symbolic! Just wait and see.[18]

Godiva is hired to seduce Leofric and coax him to lower the tax so that the citizens will have enough money to patronize the whorehouse run by the pimp Superviva and his whores the nuns. Superviva later rapes Godiva, but she comes through it untraumatized like the tough "hooer" that she is. Tom is a bus driver, whose "bus" is an elongated white wooden horse. Astride the horse he strikes Godiva-like poses and suffers sympathetically when she is attacked. Because he mimics the audience-as-voyeur, he is the least "fallen" of the characters. Near the end Godiva addresses everyone's anticipation: "For years the public has clammered [*sic*] to see more of me. This play answers their request!"[19] After putting on a long yellow wig Godiva slowly removes her clothes to striptease music. Instead of mounting Tom's horse, she uses her riding crop to coerce Superviva onto his hands and knees and rides him off the stage. Tavel's play explodes the reverential pretensions of the older legend to expose its preoccupation with Godiva's body not as an aestheticized icon, but as the target for lust. Godiva's profession of trading sex for money is merely an over-literal reading of terms that have always been part of the story: the woman's body as an erotic object, the town's marketplace, and a fiscal transaction. But within these terms it pushes the parodic inversion of the older legend to an extreme "beyond the absurd."

The film industry has made use of both the serious and the trivial strands of the Godiva legend, and it has done so exploiting the medium's capacity to shape the dynamics of the gaze. Two Hollywood films appeared in the 1950s, unremarkable except perhaps for the future screen stars they employed: *Lady Godiva Rides Again* (1951), a comedy about a beauty contest in which Joan Collins has an uncredited bit role, and *Lady Godiva* (1955) starring Maureen O'Hara, which introduced a young Clint Eastwood as the "first Saxon."[20] In the O'Hara film, Leofric and Godiva are honest, wholesome Anglo-Saxons who chafe under the policies of the invidious Norman advisers to good King Edward. Godiva agrees to the ride, first suggested by Count Eustace, to prove the loyalty of the Saxon subjects, who, she is convinced, will treat her respectfully (it is not done at the instigation of Leofric or to relieve taxes). The ride takes place in silence except for the clopping of the horse's hooves. Godiva is accompanied by an elderly nun holding (of all things) a bishop's crozier (plate 9). The town is empty, shutters are closed, with the Anglo-Saxons indoors virtuously averting their eyes while Godiva's horse can be heard passing. A scrawny Norman sympathizer named Tom, however, sneaks over to a shutter, which he opens a crack. One of the stout Saxon yeomen notices him, calls out "Tom" and blinds him with a torch. In the blinding scene the camera adopts the perspective of Tom, with the flame approaching the lens until it cuts away to a screaming Tom covering his eyes. Thus the cinema viewers are reminded of their role as voyeurs, and Tom (as always) serves as a scapegoat, receiving the punishment for the audience's voyeurism. After the blinding the camera continues to follow Godiva through her ride, part of which seems to be a *tableau vivant* of a painting by J. Lefebvre (plate 10). The film viewers, not the Saxons or Normans, are the only ones to see the naked Godiva. (In filming the scene of Godiva's naked ride, Universal Studios literally duplicated the condition of the edict forbidding Coventry's citizens from looking, when they closed off the lot from everyone except the essential personnel needed for filming.)

The viewer/voyeur identification is provocatively explored as the central theme of Michael Powell's *Peeping Tom* (1960). When it was first released, film critics "hated the piece" and their reviews ensured its failure at the box office. In recent years the critical reception has reversed itself so completely that in 1994 the film critic of London's *Sunday Times* published an apologetic retraction of her 1960 review and declared *Peeping Tom* a masterpiece.[21] Today it is acclaimed as one of the first attempts to explore the potential for violence inherent in the medium of cinema. Linda Williams, for example, comments, "Along with [Hitchcock's] *Psycho* (also 1960), it marked a significant break in the structure of the classic horror film, inaugurating a new form of psychological horror."[22] The protagonist, Mark, murders a series of women as they pose for his camera, which records their looks of terror as they die. The mechanically aided gaze, far from being passive and detached, is sadistically aggressive, "a 'devouring eye', which looks at and incorporates the external world."[23] The new form of psychological horror identified by Williams is achieved by shifting the film's point of view to that of the deranged killer, so the film-viewer-as-voyeur assumes the perspective of the voyeur-as-killer, and "we are invited to equate the art and technology of movie making with the sadist-voyeur's misuse of the female body."[24]

A much earlier and remarkable anticipation of the potential for cinema to mimic the voyeurism of the legend is found in a little-known 1927 Swedish film, *His English Wife*, directed by Gustaf Molander (better known later for Ingmar Bergman films) and starring Lil Dagover (better known for her roles in *The Cabinet of Dr. Caligari*, 1919, and *Destiny*, 1921).[25] A young Englishwoman recently married to a Swedish farmer grows increasingly distressed with her isolation in the far north. Her husband allows her to return to England for a visit, where she meets up with an old flame and goes out with him. She later agrees to help raise money for charity by riding as a bewigged Lady Godiva in a *tableau vivant* performance, but during a rehearsal her husband unexpectedly arrives and catches his wife with her old flame in an embrace backstage.

Outraged, the husband forbids her to expose her body to the public gaze, but she does so in spite of him. Eventually, after more misadventures, they are reconciled. As unpromising as the film's plot may seem, the *tableau vivant*, modeled after John Collier's painting of Godiva, is a remarkable adaptation of the new medium to the legend (plate 8). Thus Molander's film stages the voyeuristic gaze on three levels: the narrative of Lady Godiva's ride before the townspeople, Collier's painting, and the medium of film, all three of which, layered one on top of the other, compound the film viewer's role as a voyeur.

That the old legend lends itself so well to the conventions of cinema is not coincidental. The parallels are striking enough that we can use the terminology made familiar by the first generation of feminist film critics to interpret the legend in cinematic terms. Coventry's Peeping Tom sits in a darkened room, gazing anonymously through an aperture on a woman whose body is displayed in an elaborately contrived private-within-public space. In some early versions of the story he is a tailor who uses his awl to bore a hole to see the passing spectacle. His eye assumes the position of the camera lens, the projector lens, and the cinema viewer. Similarly the conventions of mainstream film, according to Laura Mulvey, "portray a hermetically sealed world which unwinds magically, indifferent to the presence of the audience, producing for them a sense of separation and playing on their voyeuristic fantasy. Moreover the extreme contrast between the darkness in the theater (which also isolates the spectators from one another) and the brilliance of the shifting patterns of light and shade on the screen helps to promote the illusion of voyeuristic separation."[26] Like the legend, which identifies the voyeur as male and even names him Tom, cinema constructs the position of the viewer as male by the conventional display of a woman's body as a sexualized object of the gaze.

To say the gaze is male is not the same as saying that only a man can adopt it. Though it is not "literally" male, E. Ann Kaplan explains, "to own and activate the gaze, given our language and the structure of the unconscious, is to be in the 'masculine' position. It is this persistent presentation of this masculine position that feminist film critics have demonstrated in their analysis of Hollywood films."[27] The male gaze is a perspective that the dominant film genres impose on every viewer, woman or man. Thus for women "trans-sex identification is a *habit* that very easily becomes *second nature*. However," Mulvey concludes somewhat incongruously, "this Nature does not sit easily and shifts restlessly in its borrowed transvestite clothes."[28]

If the pleasure of voyeurism is part of the appeal of both legend and cinema, another pleasure comes from an identification with the object of the gaze, since the one complements the other, as Freud's formulation of the scopophilic instinct makes clear.[29] According to Mulvey, "In their traditional exhibitionist role [in film] women are simultaneously looked at and displayed, with their appearance coded for strong visual and erotic impact so that they can be said to connote *to-be-looked-at-ness*."[30] If the roles of scopophiliac and exhibitionist are complementary, and if the voyeur position is available for cross-gender identification, is it possible for men to identify with the female position of exhibitionist? Mulvey is skeptical: "the male figure cannot bear the burden of sexual objectification. Man is reluctant to gaze at his exhibitionist like." Others are not so sure.[31] The two fragmentary strands into which the legend bifurcated (Peeping Tom and Lady Godiva) are reunited in Freud's complementary pairing of scopophiliac/exhibitionist, in which each position offers a possible pleasure for identification. Though the position of the voyeur is male, active, and transgressive in its gaze, it is available for identification by women; though the position of Godiva is female, passive, and the erotic object of the gaze, it is available to men. The fantasy of being beautiful, the erotic object of the gaze, and unencumbered by guilt and shame might very well have its appeal for men, even if (to paraphrase Mulvey) this Nature does not sit easily and shifts restlessly in its borrowed transvestite saddle.

While women writers have found ways to identify with Godiva's heroism since at least the Victorian period, few have attempted to recast the legend so that the woman is no longer a passive if beautiful object, vulnerable to any number of outrages. Sylvia Plath is an exception. Her 1962 poem "Ariel" rewrites the legend from the subjective point of view of the rider who breaks free of the possessive gaze of the voyeur, who is in this case the reader. At the literal level the poem describes an early morning ride on Plath's horse Ariel, as it moves from "Stasis in darkness" to a full gallop aimed like an arrow into the "red / Eye" of the rising sun.

> Stasis in darkness.
> Then the substanceless blue
> Pour of tor and distances.
>
> God's lioness,
> How one we grow,
> Pivot of heels and knees! – The furrow

Splits and passes, sister to
The brown arc
Of the neck I cannot catch,

Nigger-eye
Berries cast dark
Hooks –

Black sweet blood mouthfuls,
Shadows.
Something else

Hauls me through air –
Thighs, hair;
Flakes from my heels.

White
Godiva, I unpeel –
Dead hands, dead stringencies.

And now I
Foam to wheat, a glitter of seas.
The child's cry

Melts in the wall.
And I
Am the arrow,

The dew that flies
Suicidal, at one with the drive
Into the red

Eye, the cauldron of morning.[32]

In identifying the "I" as "White / Godiva" the poem recasts the legend to achieve a new identity by breaking free of the age-old dynamics of the gaze. The sun is not only the bullseye of a target to which the arrow flies, but also the new "I" of subjectivity. The voyeuristic male gaze is introduced through the racist image "Nigger-eye," which becomes all the more unsettling in its identification with the always voyeuristic reader, who casts looks at the rider just as the "Nigger-eye / Berries cast dark / hooks" at her white legs passing through the brambles in the pre-dawn darkness. In the violence of its racism the image inverts the usual poles of alterity, so that the gazer is made into the "other," an object defined by the commanding perspective of Godiva's gaze. Plath's "I" strikes out for freedom in an attempt to escape possession by others. Though the thorns threaten to catch her like imagined voyeurs, Plath's Godiva dashes through them and unpeels "Dead hands" of possessiveness and "dead stringencies" of obligations (the "strings" that bind her). She remains identified by her body, marked by the sexual fetishes of "Thighs, hair," which have remained remarkably consistent since the St. Albans chronicles. But liberated from the controlling gaze the body ceases to be an erotic spectacle defined by the other and asserts itself instead as the basis of its own subjectivity. The "Something else" that "hauls" her is a new paradigm of identity – God's lioness,[33] Godiva, arrow, dew. The ride is no longer the humiliating canter made at a husband's behest, for the benefit of others, and exposed to the lustful gaze of strangers. Along the way it discards the older model of contrasts (white/black, she/he, object/subject, spectacle/voyeur) in favor of something less divisive: the white/black dichotomy is supplanted by the assertion of red; the subjective "I" and the gazing "Eye" become identical; even horse and rider become unified. Though the dew flies "Suicidal" into the sun, the sun is also the "cauldron of morning," which in its ambiguity as an image holds out the possibility of transformation into a new kind of sustenance. While the awareness that Plath killed herself shortly after completing this poem makes it too easy to see the dew's flight as merely nihilistic, the dominant images throughout the poem are those of liberation and regeneration. It is intriguing to note that a Godiva procession took place in Coventry in the summer of 1962, a few months before Plath, then living in Devon, wrote "Ariel."

Plath's radical reinterpretation reminds us that, whatever else can be said about the legend, a woman's body is essential to it. Usually the body functions as the object of the gaze. However, Plath remakes Godiva into a subject who defines her environment. The disrobing is not an exposure to lustful gazes, but the peeling off of such roles. By contrast, even when the public women of Victorian England appropriated the legend and celebrated Godiva's capacity for heroic action, they maintained the older legend's patriarchal ordering of society and Godiva's role as the object of the gaze. It was empowering, perhaps, but not liberating.

If the cultural appeal of Lady Godiva has proven so durable since the thirteenth century why does it seem to be fading today? Legends do not inevitably lose their usefulness, as if they come packaged with an expiry date for consumers. Arthurian themes (to pick a similar legendary source from the Middle Ages) seem to be as robust as ever in popular culture, so when one as vigorous as the legend of Godiva begins to lose its appeal it is fair to ask why. The answer may have to do with the purposes to which the legend has been put. What values does it respond to and reinforce? What cultural work does it do? The appeal of Godiva's legend is of course much broader than an incident that may or may not have happened to an aristocratic woman from eleventh-century England.

The Godiva legend is about many things, but it always concerns the dynamics of the voyeuristic gaze – its eroticism, the position of the woman's body in a public space, and the transgressive nature of the gazing. It is helpful to think of the legend as a "theory" in the word's basic meaning of a model or conceptual frame that has explanatory power. Today there are a number of available models that do much of the same cultural work, the most notable of which is cinema, which has made the legend, as it were, the victim of an unintended side-effect of the medium. The perspective of the viewer, the position of the idealized woman's body in a contrived public space, and other affinities between the medium of cinema and the plot of the legend have made the film adaptations more than just a retelling of a quaint medieval story. They have exploited the affinities by explicitly identifying the film viewer as Peeping Tom and by staging *tableaux vivants* of other, already voyeuristic, paintings. But the similarities with the legend go beyond individual adaptations. In the most general sense, the medium constructs the perspective of the film viewer as voyeur and idealizes the display of a woman's body as the object of the gaze. The construction is not a function of any particular film or even the aggregate of all, but rather of the medium itself. Any legend would have trouble competing against such a powerful and ubiquitous institution. The cultural work the legend once did on a modest scale is now overwhelmed by the very medium of a world-wide industry.

But even if the legend has become attenuated or reduced to a simple image, it is not about to disappear. At the very least the name Godiva and the image of a naked woman on horseback are recognized around the world, even if the image resembles nothing so much as a supermodel with big hair on a horse. But even in a reduced capacity, the Godiva legend continues to persist as an instance of medievalism just as it has always done.

Medievalism, as it is understood today, is not simply a nostalgic invocation of an past culture but also a creative projection of contemporary values on it. Why are the Middle Ages the object of such fantasies more than, say, the Roman empire or the European Renaissance? For Western societies the medieval period has the advantage of being early enough to precede many of the events which have been a source of modern and postmodern anxiety: the scientific revolution, the Reformation, colonialization, industrialization, the population explosion, world wars, genocide, nuclear fission, genetic engineering, global warming – the list could go on. Despite the obvious human gains in phenomena such as industrialization, they are also seen (rightly or not) as the source of social fragmentation and personal alienation. The medieval period is remote enough that fantasies of wholeness, plenitude, and happiness can be attributed to it, yet it is also proximate enough that some continuity can be imagined to the present day. It is as if society sees itself as the adult that grew out of the childhood of the Middle Ages. Medievalism answers a yearning for larger-than-life mythical heroes. It offers a space for the irrational, for magic and miracles. It is a movement very much alive today in popular culture, from the role-playing game of "Dungeons and Dragons" to the quest plot of *Star Wars* films; from the magical parallel universe of Harry Potter to the Arthurian structure of Bernard Malamud's *The Natural*. Medievalized worlds are a staple in computer games. Society's appetite for medievalism is not limited to escapist fantasy, however. Ceremonies from the Middle Ages are still performed in courtship rituals, at university convocations, and in the courtroom. How many European countries trace their national origin to an idealized medieval event?

Those of us in the academy who work in this period like to draw a distinction between medievalism on the one hand and the more serious business of medieval studies, which is what we practice.[34] According to this distinction (and with some ironic exaggeration) medieval studies is pursued through the interpretation of empirical evidence guided by established methodologies. It has access to the real Middle Ages through old texts and other artifacts. By contrast, medievalism picks and chooses from the hard-won conclusions of medieval studies, using their gleanings as a means to a more frivolous end. What Charles Kingsley had to say about Godiva was an example of Victorian medievalism, which irritated the professional historian Edward Freeman. The distinction is even reflected in the material discussed in this book: the first chapter pursues a medieval studies agenda, while the others trace an extensive episode of medievalism. Even within the profession the distinction from medievalism is not always so sharp. When a literary scholar reconstructs the audience for an early poem, how much of it is an anachronistic projection? And how can we tell? Many scholars find medieval studies appealing because the vacillation between the familiar and the strange elicits a combination of intellectual and imaginative responses in the attempt to understand the past. The imaginative in this case is not the same as escapist fantasy, though they have something in common. When I find myself surprised by the uncanny in medieval literature, I begin to look with a more discerning eye on my everyday world.

Roger of Wendover and Matthew Paris were accomplished historians who would have been puzzled by the distinctions I have outlined here. While their historiography was as serious as any modern scholar's, they would be less bothered by the mixing of the idealistic and real, because history to them consisted in the unfolding of a providential design, which itself was the greatest of ideals. So their chronicles could mingle what we now consider fiction and fact as long as the higher goal of historiography was served. What is unusual (though not unique) in the case of Godiva is how they fashioned an early instance of medievalism. They were not very far removed from Godiva, who lived less than 200 years earlier and fewer than 100 miles away. Yet in the interval between her death and the 1230s, society had changed so radically that they were able to idealize Anglo-Saxon England as a bygone culture, where a woman could make a dramatic gesture in pursuit of a noble cause. Or, more precisely, they imagined a place where a fictive thirteenth-century woman could make such a dramatic gesture. Every later version down through the centuries has continued to interpret Godiva as a contemporary inhabiting a medievalized fantasy world. Perhaps the best illustration of the legend's medievalism can be found in the dynamics of its own plot. Just as Peeping Tom projects sexual fantasies onto the naked body of Godiva, medievalism projects imaginary virtues on a past culture. But the analogy suggests its obverse, because just as Godgifu's body had a flesh-and-blood existence before it became legendary, the Middle Ages cannot be reduced simply to an imaginative construct, like a castle in the sky. Godiva's ride has never really been about the eleventh-century woman named Godgifu. She would never be able to imagine, not in a thousand years, what others have fantasized through the legend of Lady Godiva.

Notes

Chapter 1 Godgifu of Mercia

1   This chapter will identify her using the Old English name Godgifu. Although her birth date is unknown, an age in the mid-fifties at death would be a reasonable assumption, judging from the time of her marriage (before 1035) and from the approximate age of her son Ælfgar. From the West Saxon royal line: Æthelred, Edmund, Edward the Confessor; from the Danish line Swein Forkbeard, Cnut, Harold Harefoot, Harthacnut; from the Godwine family Harold; and from the Normans William the Conqueror.

2   See William of Malmesbury, *Gesta Regum Anglorum*, vol. i, p. 717. Matilda's baptized name was another Old English compound, Eadgyth (Edith); see the *DNB* under Henry I (p. 441). King Æthelred's daughter was also named Godgifu; see Stenton, *Anglo-Saxon England*, p. 560.

3   Stenton, *Anglo-Saxon England*, p. 395.

4   Æthelred's nickname does not appear in surviving contemporary sources, though it likely enjoyed an oral circulation.

5   *ASC*, p. 93.

6   Translated in *EHD I*, pp. 928–43.

7   Fleming, *Kings and Lords in Conquest England*, pp. 70–2. See also Stenton, *Anglo-Saxon England*, pp. 416–17.

8   Stenton, *Anglo-Saxon England*, p. 417.

9   The summary below draws from the following sources: Fleming, *Kings and Lords in Conquest England*; Lancaster, *Godiva*; and Stenton, *Anglo-Saxon England*.

10   *ASC*, p. 134.

11   *John of Worcester*, pp. 582–3. The most detailed early sources for Leofric are this chronicle (for many years mistakenly attributed to Florence of Worcester) and the D-text of the *Anglo-Saxon Chronicle*, both with Worcester connections. See John, "The End of Anglo-Saxon England," p. 222, for a discussion of their biases and relation.

12 *ASC*, pp. 420–1.

13 *John of Worcester*, pp. 532–3.

14 Ibid., pp. 534–5.

15 Ibid., pp. 544–5.

16 Ibid., pp. 560–1, 570–1, 572–3.

17 *History of the Norman Conquest of England*, vol. ii, p. 268.

18 *John of Worcester*, p. 583.

19 Napier, "An Old English Vision of Leofric Earl of Mercia," pp. 180–7. The Old English reads: *Feowertyne nihton ær his forðsiðe he foresæde þone dæg þe he sceolde cuman to Cofantreo to his langan hame, þær he on restet; and hit aeode eall swa he sæde.* Ker, *A Catalogue of Manuscripts Containing Anglo-Saxon*, no. 64, dates the manuscript "s. xi med., xi²," which would put it within decades after Leofric's death. For the date of the fleet at Sandwich see Stenton, *Anglo-Saxon England*, pp. 427–9.

20 Paris, *La Estoire de Seint Aedward le Rei*, lines 2514–97 and 4927–38. The manuscript is Cambridge University Library MS Ee.3.59. Facsimiles of the manuscript pages including the illustrations are available for viewing at the Cambridge University Library website with discussion by Paul Binski: http://www.lib.cam.ac.uk.

21 *Anglo-Saxon Charters*, ed. Robertson, p. 461, summarizes the evidence from Heming's Cartulary. See also Lancaster, *Godiva*, pp. 41 and 18, where she concludes, "In all, Leofric and his family acted with extraordinary uncharitableness towards the abbey and cathedral at Worcester. There is no apparent reason for this."

22 *Chronicon Abbatiae de Evesham*, ed. Macray, pp. 83–5.

23 *EHD I*, p. 466.

24 "Maxims I," in *The Exeter Book*, ed. Krapp and Dobbie, p. 160, line 100.

25 *EHD I*, p. 467.

26 *Anglo-Saxon Charters*, ed. Robertson, pp. 212, 210.

27 The Old English is conveniently printed in *Sweet's Anglo-Saxon Reader*, ed. Whitelock, pp. 57–8, and translated by Whitelock in *EHD I*, pp. 602–3. Stafford, "Women and the Norman Conquest," gives a more skeptical interpretation of the extent of women's legal rights in pre-Conquest England.

28 Gover, Mawer, and Stenton, *The Place Names of Warwickshire*, p. 172. See Stenton, "The Historical Bearing of Place-Name Studies: The Place of Women in Anglo-Saxon Society."

29 *EHD II*, pp. 858–64.

30 *EHD II*, p. 858.

31 Harold's "official" wife, at least in the eyes of the Church, was Ealdgifu, the daughter of Earl Ælfgar and granddaughter of Leofric and Godgifu, whom he married in 1063. Gytha's property was valued at £588 and Eadgifu the Fair's at £366 in 1066, according to the figures in Clarke, *The English Nobility under Edward the Confessor*, pp. 14, 32, 56–8. On the motivation to un-

derestimate the amount of land owned by women in both 1066 and 1086, see Stafford, "Women in Domesday," pp. 81 and 85.

32 See the relevant discussion for a queen's title in Stafford, *Queen Emma and Queen Edith*, pp. 55–64.

33 *Anglo-Saxon Charters*, ed. Robertson, no. 19. For a summary of Æthelflæd's career and the difficulty of sources, see Wainwright, "Æthelflæd, Lady of the Mercians."

34 A similar instance from American history would be Edith, the wife of President Woodrow Wilson, who took over much of the executive decision-making after Woodrow was incapacitated by a stroke in 1919. But Edith, unlike Æthelflæd, had to conceal her role. For Æthelflæd see Fell, *Women in Anglo-Saxon England*, p. 91.

35 "Dei cultrix, sancteque Marie semper uirginis amatrix deuota, nobilis comitissa Godgiua," *John of Worcester*, pp. 582–3.

36 *Chronicon Abbatiæ de Evesham*, ed. Macray, pp. 83–5.

37 Walter of Coventry claimed that Leofric and Godiva founded the monastery from their own patrimony (*de suo patrimonio*), which suggests she came from a wealthy family; see his *Memoriale Fratris*, p. 72. Other evidence is summarized in Lancaster, *Godiva*, pp. 19–20. Though the charter is a fourteenth-century forgery, the detail about Thorold's relation to Godgifu would lend credence to the document only if it were generally known to be true.

38 Lancaster, *Godiva*, pp. 22–3, summarizes the evidence from the Domesday Book. For Godgifu's possessions in Warwickshire see "Text of the Warwickshire Domesday," ed. and trans. Carter, pp. 309–10.

39 *Anglo-Saxon Charters*, ed. Robertson, pp. 210–11.

40 Ibid., pp. 212–17; Stenton, *Anglo-Saxon England*, p. 438. For a list of their grants, see *John of Worcester*, p. 583, and the discussion in Lancaster, *Godiva*, pp. 33–42.

41 Fleming, *Kings and Lords in Conquest England*, 58; *John of Worcester*, p. 583. Godgifu seems to have given the land for the monastery itself, and Leofric endowed it with more for its maintenance.

42 Dugdale, *The Antiquities of Warwickshire*, p. 100n.

43 See Heslop, "The Production of *de luxe* Manuscripts and the Patronage of King Cnut and Queen Emma," p. 185.

44 Orderic Vitalis, *The Ecclesiastical History*, vol. ii, p. 217.

45 On Mannig see *Chronicon Abbatiae de Evesham*, ed. Macray, p. 86; William of Malmesbury, *Gesta Pontificum Anglorum*, pp. 309–11. On Limesey see Lancaster, "The Coventry Forged Charters," pp. 134–5.

46 Hill, *An Atlas of Anglo-Saxon England*, figs. 248 and 249.

47 "Maxims I," p. 159, line 63.

48 See Owen-Crocker, *Dress in Anglo-Saxon England*, ch. 7.

49 *Anglo-Saxon Wills*, ed. Whitelock, pp. 14–15.

50 Quoted from Fell, "A 'friwif locbore' Revisited," p. 164.

51 *Beowulf*, ed. Mitchell and Robinson, lines 994–6.

52 *Hemingi Chartularium Ecclesiae Wigorniensis*, ed. Hearne, vol i, pp. 261–2, quoted in *Anglo-Saxon Charters*, ed. Robertson, p. 461. Heming, who describes Edwin and Morcar's seizure of land as *instinctu diabolico*, is biased in favor of the church in Worcester. Ælfgar had another son, Beorhtric, about whom little is known.

53 See Beech, "England and Aquitaine in the Century before the Norman Conquest," pp. 94–5.

Chapter 2 Godiva Emerges

1 Translated by the author from *Chronica Majora*, vol. i, pp. 526–7. Even though Matthew Paris lived and wrote a generation after Roger of Wendover, the manuscript from which this version comes (Cambridge Corpus Christi College 26) is the earliest, "produced under the direct supervision of Matthew Paris" (Vaughan, *Matthew Paris*, p. 21).

2 1 Corinthians 11: 15, "mulier vero si comam nutriat, gloria est illi: quoniam capilli pro velamine ei dati sunt," *Biblia Vulgata; The Holy Bible*, Douai/Rheims translation.

3 For a perceptive discussion of the symbolism of Godiva's nakedness and hair, see French, "The Legend of Lady Godiva and the Image of the Female Body," pp. 16–17. For hair as an erotic ornament see Hollander, *Seeing Through Clothes*, pp. 73–5, 184–5, and passim.

4 Voragine, *The Golden Legend*, vol. i, p. 24.

5 Karras, *Common Women*, p. 15.

6 Farmer, *The Oxford Dictionary of Saints*, pp. 194–5.

7 Symonds, *Wine, Women and Song*, p. 68: "Si ponas Hippolytum hodie Papiae, / non erit Hippolytus in sequenti die." Quoted from *The Oxford Book of Medieval Latin Verse*, ed. Raby, p. 264.

8 *The Riverside Chaucer*, ed. Benson, pp. 148–9.

9 See Spearing, *The Medieval Poet as Voyeur*; Stanbury, "The Voyeur and the Private Life in Troilus and Criseyde," p. 141, and "The Virgin's Gaze: Spectacle and Transgression in Middle English Lyrics of the Passion."

10 Brett, "John of Worcester and his Contemporaries," p. 101.

11 Campbell, "Some Twelfth-Century Views of the Anglo-Saxon Past," p. 142.

12 See Brett, "John of Worcester and his Contemporaries," p. 106, who dates its arrival in Coventry before 1200. The manuscript is Trinity College, Dublin, MS 502.

13 See Vaughan, *Matthew Paris*, pp. 21–34. The relevant editions are Roger of Wendover, *Chronica sive Flores Historiarum*, vol. i, p. 497, and *Chronica Majora*, vol. i, p. 576.

14 Vaughan, *Matthew Paris*, p. 12.

15 Ibid., p. 152.

16 Parker left the Godiva story unrevised. The quotation is taken from the article on Matthew Paris by W. Hunt in the *DNB*; see also Vaughan, *Matthew Paris*, pp. 152–4.

17 Taken from Vaughan, *Matthew Paris*, p. 33.

18 Brooke, *From Alfred to Henry III*, p. 4; Vaughan, *Matthew Paris*, pp. 125–58; and the article by Hunt in the *DNB*.

19 See Hartland, "Peeping Tom and Lady Godiva," and Liebrecht, *Zur Volkskunde*, p. 104. See also Graves, *The White Goddess*, p. 401.

20 Davidson, "The Ride: In Folk Tradition," p. 63.

21 See Mac Cana, *Celtic Mythology*, pp. 51, 81, 89. The passage is quoted from *The Mabinogi*, ed. and trans. Ford, p. 42.

22 See Davidson, "The Ride: In Folk Tradition," p. 69, who mentions a parallel with Aslaug in the *Saga of Ragnar Lodbrok*.

23 See Burbidge, pp. 42–3, and Davidson, "The Ride: In Folk Tradition," p. 64.

24 Such a sequence of steps is in Bolton, "The Legend of Lady Godiva," pp. 245–7. See also Graves, *The White Goddess*.

25 This theory was first advanced by J. G. Wood in the introduction to his edition of Waterton, *Wanderings in South America*; see also Waterton, "Hereward le Wake: The Countess Lucy," p. 31

26 Bartlett, *England under the Norman and Angevin Kings*, p. 162.

27 See Lancaster, *Godiva*, p. 45. For a summary of national taxation see Loyn, *The Governance of Anglo-Saxon England, 500–1087*, pp. 118–22.

28 "Text of the Warwickshire Domesday," ed. and trans. Carter, p. 310.

29 Coss, *Lordship, Knighthood and Locality*, p. 26.

30 Lancaster, "The Coventry Forged Charters," p. 114.

31 *The Early Records of Medieval Coventry*, ed. Coss, pp. xvii–xix. See also Davis, "The Early History of Coventry," p. 19.

32 Lancaster, "The Coventry Forged Charters," p. 129.

33 *Grafton's Chronicle*, pp. 147–8.

34 Quoted from an early edition based on one of Grafton's printed copies, *The Chronicle of John Hardyng*, ed. Ellis, p. 231. The readings of an early manuscript, London, British Library Harleian 661, are restored, with one exception: Grafton's *redeme* for the Harleian's *remedie*.

35 Brompton's version is conveniently reprinted in *Bishop Percy's Folio MS*, ed. Hales and Furnivall, vol. iii, pp. 473–4, though the editors incorrectly place Brompton in the twelfth century.

36 Higden, *Polychronicon*, vol. vii, pp. 198–200.

Chapter 3 Godiva's Progress

1 Quoted from Burbidge, pp. 52–3. The first sentence is a paraphrase of Dugdale, *The Antiquities of Warwickshire*, p. 116. The earliest version that I

have seen was transcribed in a letter by T. B. Bruckfield of 1813, now in the Fretton Collection the Coventry City Records office. I am grateful to Ron Aquilla Clarke of the Herbert Art Gallery and Museums for a photocopy of the letter.

2   Burbidge, p. 51, Clarke and Day, p. 16.

3   Until recent years it was thought to be a statue of St. George, but more recently that identification has been thrown into question (R. A. Clarke, personal communication). St. George was the patron saint of England, who according to one tradition was born near Coventry.

4   See Stephens, ed., *A History of the County of Warwick*, vol. viii: *The City of Coventry and Borough of Warwick*, p. 219. Although the eucharist remained a sacrament, the second Prayer Book of 1552 shifted the congregation's focus away from it by eliminating processions and the elevation. See Duffy, *The Stripping of the Altars*, p. 464. Henry VIII affirmed the doctrine of transubstantiation in the Ten Articles of 1536, though Edward VI's Forty-Two Articles of 1553 regard it as "repugnant to the plain words of scripture" (article XXIX, later becoming XXVIII); see Dickens, *The English Reformation*, pp. 174–6, 253.

5   It is also worth noting that this period saw the invention of pornography. See Hunt, "Introduction: Obscenity and the Origins of Modernity, 1500–1800."

6   The Cappers guild kept possession of their pageant wagon until 1630 (Ingram, REED, p. 430). As late as 1866 a visitor to Coventry reports that the procession had wagons, on which were painted "many forms and scenes which I could trace to [*sic*] through a succession of pageants and moralities back to the original 'Mysteries' of Coventry": Conway, "Lady Godiva At Home," p. 632.

7   See Rubin, *Corpus Christi: The Eucharist in Late Medieval Culture*.

8   Ingram, REED, p. 71. See also Harris, *Life in an Old English Town*, pp. 340–1, and Sharp, *Dissertation*, pp. 165–7.

9   On processions see Phythian-Adams, "Ceremony and the Citizen: The Communal Year at Coventry 1450–1550"; see also James, "Ritual, Drama and Social Body in the Late Medieval English Town."

10   Ingram, REED, p. xxii; Phythian-Adams, "Ceremony and the Citizen," p. 58.

11   Recent studies have shifted emphasis away from the optimistic view of Phythian-Adams and Mervyn James to emphasize the power relations embedded in processions. See Rubin, *Corpus Christi*, pp. 248–73; Beckwith, *Signifying God*; and Lindebaum, "Ceremony and Oligarchy: The London Midsummer Watch."

12   *Johannis de Fordun Scotichronicon Genuinum*, ed. Hearnes, vol. v, p. 1443.

13   Rubin (*Corpus Christi*, p. 233) characterizes religious fraternities: "Let us try to understand fraternities as providers of essential personal, familial, religious, economic and political services, as providing security in some essen-

tial areas of life; and let us see these activities as articulated most frequently in symbols from the language of religion."

14 Quoted from Sharp, *Dissertation*, p. 170.

15 "Behind the repudiation of ceremonial by the reformers lay a radically different conceptual world, a world in which text was everything, sign nothing. The sacramental universe of late medieval Catholicism was, from such a perspective, totally opaque, a bewildering and meaningless world of dumb objects and vapid gestures, hindering communication": Duffy, *The Stripping of the Altars*, p. 532.

16 "The cult of Gloriana was skilfully created to buttress public order, and even more, deliberately to replace the pre-Reformation externals of religion, the cult of the Virgin and saints with their attendant images, processions, ceremonies and secular rejoicing": Strong, *The Cult of Elizabeth*, p. 16.

17 *The Coventry Corpus Christi Plays*, ed. King and Davidson. For a survey of recent scholarship see Johnston, "'All the World was a Stage'."

18 *A Hundred Merry Tales and other English Jest-books of the Fifteenth and Sixteenth Centuries*, ed. Zall; quoted from Duffy, *The Stripping of the Altars*, p. 68.

19 Coventry City Annals, as quoted in Ingram, REED, p. 294.

20 Gardiner, *Mysteries' End*, p. 72, and ch. 5 passim.

21 *The Towneley Plays*, ed. Stevens and Cawley, vol. i, pp. xxiv, 224.

22 Foxe, *Acts and Monuments of Martyrs*, vol. ii, p. 1920 col. b – p. 1921 col. a; quoted from Ingram, REED, p. 207.

23 Dugdale, *The Antiquities of Warwickshire*, p. 116.

24 See Ingram, REED, under the relevant years. For the Shakespearean lore see *The Coventry Leet Book*, ed. Harris, pt. 4, pp. xlix–l.

25 See Phythian-Adams, *Desolation of a City*, esp. pp. 31–51, 281.

26 See also Burbidge, p. 55, for a reference to a procession to open the Great Fair in 1645, though there is no mention of a Godiva impersonator.

27 In a way the Godiva procession satirizes *all* processions, religious and secular, because the presence of physical bodies is essential to their rhetoric. What Godiva presents to the crowd, however, is not a real body but a simulacrum: the impersonator's body is disguised as another that offers itself as more "authentic" (i.e. naked) but which of course is fake.

28 *The Coventry Leet Book*, ed. Harris, p. 57; Burbidge, p. 38.

29 Ingram, REED, p. 577, who continues: "Soon thereafter she was replaced by the more neutral plaque of the king's coat of arms."

30 Lancaster, *Godiva*, pp. 56–60; Burbidge, pp. 55–63; Clarke and Day, p. 28. In recent years the city of Coventry has revived a festive Godiva procession, which has no association with the earlier religious occasions.

31 Phythian-Adams, *Desolation of a City*, p. 171.

32 Dugdale, *The Antiquities of Warwickshire*, p. 86. The evidence is summarized by Burbidge, pp. 46–8.

33 See Lancaster, *Godiva*, pp. 50–1.

34 *The Coventry Leet Book*, ed. Harris, p. 567.

35 Ingram, REED, lists "Ives distaffe" in the 1591 inventory of the Cappers' guild. In the conventions of medieval drama, her role was likely played by a man or boy.

36 See Delony, *Works*, pp. 309–11 and notes; this edition, by F. O. Mann, is of a 1631 printing.

37 *A Collection of Old Ballads*, vol. ii, pp. 34–8. It was also transcribed into the mid-seventeenth-century manuscript that was published by Thomas Percy as *Reliques of Ancient English Poetry* in 1765; for a modern edition see *Bishop Percy's Folio MS*, ed. Hales and Furnivall, vol. iii, pp. 473–7.

38 Quoted here from *Bishop Percy's Folio MS*.

39 A chorographic poem proceeds from region to region, as if moving across a map. For a discussion of *Poly-Olbion* see Helgerson, *Forms of Nationhood in the Elizabethan Writings of England*, p. 128. The Drayton quotation is from the *DNB* under the entry for Deloney.

40 Drayton, *Works*, vol. ii, p. 282.

41 Phythian-Adams, *Desolation of a City*, p. 80.

42 Rubin, *Corpus Christi*, p. 270.

43 See the transcription of the City Annals by Burbidge, p. 256. On the queer space this substitution opens up see Stallybrass, "Transvestism and the 'Body Beneath'."

44 See Baldwin, *Sumptuary Legislation*, p. 249. For a recent survey see Hunt, *Governance of the Consuming Passions*.

45 Hollander, *Seeing Through Clothes*, pp. 205–6. For the collarbone measurements, see Hunt, *Governance of the Consuming Passions*, pp. 221–2, who speculates on "the coexistence of the tendencies that make women more modest and more exhibitionist, in that both their shame and their attractiveness relate to the whole body. The greater diffusion of female sexuality ensures the persistent ambiguity that marks women's existence between sexual exhibitionism and modesty."

46 Boileau, *A Just and Seasonable Reprehension*, p. 3.

47 Ibid., pp. 143–4.

48 Jago, "Edge-Hill," in *Works of the English Poets*, ed. Chalmers, p. 296.

49 Ibid., p. 297.

50 The following anecdotes are drawn primarily from Burbidge, pp. 55–63.

51 Collins, *Brief Reflections*, quoted from Häfele, *Die Godivasage*, p. 36.

52 Quoted with regularized spelling and punctuation from the Longfellow Journal MS Am 1340 (184), 1829–30, p. 10, in the Houghton Library of Harvard University. I am grateful to Kathleen Verduin for this reference.

53 Burbidge, p. 58.

54 Ibid., pp. 56, 58; Lancaster, *Godiva*, p. 58; Poole, *Coventry: Its History and Antiquities*, p. 65.

Chapter 4 Peeping Tom

1 *Grafton's Chronicle*, p. 148.
2 *A Relation of A Short Survey of Twenty-Six Counties*, ed. Wickham Legg, p. 70.
3 Ibid.
4 Clarke and Day, p. 16.
5 The emergence of Peeping Tom in the mid-seventeenth century would seem to be at least distantly related to the proliferation of sumptuary laws (see the last chapter) and to the invention of pornography. See Hunt, "Introduction: Obscenity and the Origins of Modernity, 1500–1800."
6 See Clarke and Day, p. 16; Burbidge, pp. 50–4. Lancaster, *Godiva*, p. 54, also quotes from a City Annal from the second half of the seventeenth century, which recounts how "one desirous to see the strange Case lett downe a Window, & looked out" when he heard Godiva's horse neigh.
7 Quoted from Burbidge, p. 52. An anonymous pamphlet published after 1842 says "[o]f late years the wig has been discontinued": *The History of Coventry Show Fair*, p. 6.
8 *A Collection of Old Ballads*, vol. ii, p. 36.
9 Samuel Butler's *Hudibras* of 1663 plays off the proverb in the couplet, "Compos'd of many Ingredient Valors / Just like the Manhood of nine Taylors": *Hudibras*, ed. Wilders, I. ii. 22. See also *tailor* n. B.1.b in the *OED* and the citations there.
10 Davies, *Journal of the Very Reverend Rowland Davies*, p. 104. Defoe, *A Tour Thro' the Whole Island of Great Britain*, vol. ii, p. 483.
11 "Edge Hill," in *Works of the English Poets*, ed. Chalmers, p. 296. For more discussion of this poem see pp. 66–7.
12 Victoria is quoted from Lennie, *Landseer: The Victorian Paragon*, p. 209. Stephens, *Sir Edwin Landseer*, p. 107.
13 Hollander, *Seeing Through Clothes*, p. 178.
14 "The Sexual Aberrations," in *Three Essays on the Theory of Sexuality*, p. 157. The reference to Godiva and Peeping Tom is in *The Psycho-Analytic View of Psychogenic Disturbance of Vision*, p. 217.
15 Sartre, *Being and Nothingness*, p. 277.

Chapter 5 Godiva Domesticated

1 See Ferguson with Stoney, *Victoria and Albert*, pp. 123–4. For a photograph see Smith, *Exposed*, p. 75. The Godiva statue was commissioned from Émile Jeannest (a Paris-trained sculptor working in Birmingham), and is now in the Armoury of Windsor Castle. On Victoria's gifts see Weintraub, *Victoria*, p. 239.
2 Francis Charles Augustus Emmanuel Albert, *Letters of the Prince Consort, 1831–1861*, ed. Jagow, p. 275. See also Richardson, *Victoria and Albert*, pp. 184–7;

Hough, *Victoria and Albert*, pp. 148–9.

3   Duby, *A History of Private Life*, vol ii, p. ix.

4   Ruskin, *Sesame and Lilies*, pp. 89–90.

5   These include reviews in the *Examiner, The Monthly Review*, and *The Morning Herald*, as well as a number in America, which increased the poem's availability to the general public well beyond the initial 500 copies of the book sold. See Shannon, *Tennyson and the Reviewers*, pp. 60–9. Before copies of Tennyson's *Poems* of 1842 reached American bookstores, "Godiva" was printed in the journal *Brother Jonathan* and spread from there to newssheets. See Eidson, *Tennyson in America*, pp. 40 and 212 n. 21.

6   See Culler, *The Poetry of Tennyson*, p. 112. Quotations are from *Poems of Tennyson*, ed. Ricks, vol. ii.

7   This line is the earliest attestation of the phrase in the *OED*, which, along with "hang around," was considered colloquial.

8   See *Poems of Tennyson*, pp. 174–5.

9   See also Christ, "The Feminine Subject in Victorian Poetry," p. 386.

10 Leigh Hunt, unsigned review, *Church of England Quarterly Review*, 12 (Oct. 1842), pp. 361–76, quoted from Jump, ed., *Tennyson: The Critical Heritage*, p. 127.

11 Jump, ed., *Tennyson: The Critical Heritage*, p. 133.

12 Ibid., p. 136.

13 Quoted from Hunt, *Tales*, p. 169; first published in *Indicator*, 3, 27 Oct. 1819, pp. 16–19, it was later published as a book in his collection of essays also entitled *Indicator* (London, 1822).

14 Landor, *Imaginary Conversations*, vol. ii, pp. 519–20.

15 Quoted from Hunt, *Poetical Works*, p. 79.

16 Portions of it are published by W. Hickling in *History and Antiquities of the City of Coventry*, pp. 4–6, and in Conway, "Lady Godiva At Home," p. 632 (who describes the Coventry minstrels).

17 Hawkes, *A Brief History of the Earl of Mercia, Lady Godiva, and Peeping Tom of Coventry*.

18 Quotations are from Mermin, *Godiva's Ride*, pp. xvi and 20.

19 See Egan, "Glad Rags for Lady Godiva."

20 Butler, *The New Godiva*, pp. 27–8 (published anonymously).

21 Walkowitz, *Prostitution and Victorian Society*, pp. 114–15.

22 Crary, *Techniques of the Observer*, p. 9. See also Marsh, "Spectacle."

23 For reproductions see Lancaster, *Godiva*; Häfele, *Die Godivasage*; Clarke and Day; and Kirby, "In Memory of Lady Godiva." For a chronological listing of artwork from all periods, see Clarke and Day, pp. 30ff.

24 Clark, *The Nude*. See also Hollander, *Seeing Through Clothes*, pp. 157–207, and Berger et al., *Ways of Seeing*, pp. 47–54.

25 Quoted from Woolner, *Thomas Woolner R. A., Sculptor and Poet*, p. 307.

26 On Victorian classicism see Jenkyns, *Dignity and Decadence*, esp. ch. 5, "Hellene High Water," and Smith, *The Victorian Nude*.

27 Performed on 6 Sept. 1784; published 1785 as *Peeping Tom; or the Coventry Magistrates: A Comic Opera in Two Acts*, score by Samuel Arnold.
28 Ibid., p. 8.
29 Wolcot, "The Convention Bill; Ode To Mr. Pitt," lines 71–6, in *The Works of Peter Pindar*; the verse was first published as a quarto in 1795.
30 See Gifford, "The Etonian," p. 106. Wordsworth identifies him as "Moutray" in a letter to Henry Crabb Robinson; quoted from *The Critical Opinions of William Wordsworth*, ed. Peacock, p. 316.
31 *The Poems of Tennyson*, vol. ii, pp. 174–5.
32 By Francis Talfourd and W. P. Hale, the play was published in London by H. Lacy.
33 Freeman, *Old English History for Children*, p. 279; *History of the Norman Conquest of England*, vol. ii, p. 31. Freeman began his *History for Children* in 1860. Both works sold well and went through several revisions.
34 Kingsley, *Hereward the Wake*, pp. 28–9. For the opinion of Max Müller and others see the entry in the *DNB* under Kingsley.
35 Stubbs, *Historical Memorials of Ely Cathedral*, p. 1.
36 *Hereward the Wake*, p. 9n.
37 *Saturday Review*, 6 Apr. 1895, pp. 443–5. Shaw notes that the "living picture" of Godiva was modeled after the 1870 painting by Frans Joseph van Lerius, in which she is seen emerging into a hallway while clutching a drape to conceal her nakedness.

Chapter 6 Godiva Displayed

1 *The Seven Lady Godivas*, pages unnumbered.
2 See Morgan and Morgan, *Dr. Seuss and Mr. Geisel*, p. 93.
3 *The Psycho-Analytic View of Psychogenic Disturbance of Vision*, p. 219.
4 *Instincts and their Vicissitudes*, pp. 129ff.
5 "And then there was Maude," lyrics by Dave Grusin and Andrew Bergman.
6 "History of the Company," distributed by Godiva Chocolatier, 1993.
7 From the Associated Press, 2 Aug. 1996.
8 "Lady Godiva," in *History of British Rock*, vol. iv, R2 70322, S2 57812.
9 Reuters, 18 Jan. 1996.
10 Rivas, *Lady Godiva: Leyenda historica*; Frida, [*Legendy*]: *Sv. Vojtech, Godiva, Armida, Trilogie or Simsonovi*; Maeterlinck, *Monna Vanna*.
11 For a summary see Häfele, *Die Godivasage*, pp. 111–14, 151–75, 222–86. To these can be added Max Mell's "Lady Godiva."
12 In Auden, *About the House*, p. 32.
13 Moravia, *Lady Godiva and Other Stories*.
14 Faure, *Lady Godiva and Master Tom*, p. 39.
15 Ibid., p. 138.

16 DeMott, "Cathy Ames and Lady Godiva."

17 Sowden, *Lady of Coventry*, p. 315.

18 Tavel, "The Life of Lady Godiva, an Hysterical Drama," p. 181.

19 Ibid., p. 200.

20 Robert Arthur (producer) and Arthur Lubin (director), Universal City, California: Universal Pictures, 1955, 1983.

21 Marks, *Peeping Tom*, pp. xxiv–xxv.

22 Williams, "When the Woman Looks," p. 90. An element of Powell's cinematic project that seems to be absent from the Godiva legend is "the narcissistic mirror that the cinematic apparatus holds up" to the woman victim, who in looking at the camera lens sees herself as an exhibitionist (p. 93).

23 Fenichel, "The Scopophilic Instinct and Identification," p. 32.

24 Williams, "When the Woman Looks," p. 92.

25 *Hans Engelska Fru*, produced by Oscar Hemberg; it was released in England as *Matrimony* and in the United States as *Discord*.

26 Mulvey, "Visual Pleasure and the Narrative Cinema," p. 17; see also Kaplan, "Is the Gaze Male?"

27 Kaplan, "Is the Gaze Male?", p. 30.

28 Mulvey, "Afterthoughts," p. 33; emphasis hers.

29 *Instincts and their Vicissitudes*, p. 129.

30 Mulvey, "Visual Pleasure and the Narrative Cinema," p. 19. See, more recently, Solomon-Godeau, "The Legs of the Countess," p. 306.

31 Mulvey, "Visual Pleasure and the Narrative Cinema," p. 20. For the possibility of cross-gender identification, see Clover, *Men, Women, and Chain Saws*, p. 40.

32 *Ariel*, pp. 26–7. For another, more recent, poetic interpretation, see María Victoria Atencia's "Godiva en blue jean," in *Antología Poética*, p. 119.

33 "Ariel" means "God's lion."

34 A great deal has been written on medievalism in recent years, but still valuable is the ten-part anatomy in Eco, "Dreaming of the Middle Ages," pp. 61–72. For a perceptive summary of the legacy of Anglo-Saxon England, see Shippey, "The Undeveloped Image: Anglo-Saxon in Popular Consciousness from Turner to Tolkien," pp. 215–36.

Bibliography

Primary Sources

Albert, Francis Charles Augustus Emmanuel, *Letters of the Prince Consort, 1831–1861*, trans. E. T. S. Dugdale, ed. Kurt Jagow. London: Murray, 1938.

Anglo-Saxon Charters, ed. A. J. Robertson. Cambridge: Cambridge University Press, 1956.

Anglo-Saxon Charters, ed. P. H. Sawyer. London: Royal Historical Society, 1968.

Anglo-Saxon Chronicle, ed. Dorothy Whitelock, D. C. Douglas, and S. I. Tucker. New Brunswick: Rutgers University Press, 1961.

Anglo-Saxon Wills, ed. Dorothy Whitelock. Cambridge: Cambridge University Press, 1930.

Anglo-Saxon Writs, with "A Bromfield and Coventry Writ of King Edward the Confessor" (1959) ed. Florence E. Harmer. 1952; repr. Stamford: Paul Watkins, 1989.

Atencia, María Victoria, *Antología Poética*, ed. José Luis García Martín. Madrid: Castalia, 1990.

Auden, W. H., *About the House*. New York: Random House, 1965.

Beowulf: An Edition, ed. Bruce Mitchell and Fred C. Robinson. Oxford: Blackwell, 1998.

Biblia Vulgata; Biblia Sacra juxta Vulgatam Clementinam, ed. Alberto Colunga and Laurentio Turrado, 6th edn. Madrid: Biblioteca de Autores Cristianos, 1977

Binsky, Paul, *Facsimile of Cambridge University Library MS Ee.3.59*. 1997. Website: <http://www.lib.cam.ac.uk>.

Bishop Percy's Folio MS: Ballads and Romances, ed. J. W. Hales and F. J. Furnivall, vol. iii. London: N. Trübner & Co., 1868.

Boileau, Jacques, *A Just and Seasonable Reprehension of Naked Breasts and Shoulders Written by a Grave and Learned Papist*, trans. Edward Cooke. London: Jonathan Edwin, 1678.

Bradshaw, Henry, *The Holy Lyfe and History of Saynt Werburge*. Manchester: Chetham Society, 1848.

Butler, Josephine, *The New Godiva: A Dialogue*. London: Isbister, 1883.

Butler, Samuel, *Hudibras*, ed. John Wilders. Oxford: Clarendon Press, 1967.

Chaucer, Geoffrey, *The Riverside Chaucer*, ed. Larry D. Benson. Boston: Houghton Mifflin, 1987.

Chronicon Abbatiae de Evesham, ad annum 1418, ed. W. D. Macray. London: Longman, Green, 1863.

A Collection of Old Ballads: Corrected from the Best and Most Ancient Copies Extant; With Introductions Historical, Critical, or Humorous, vol. ii. London: printed for J. Roberts and sold by J. Brotherton, A. Bettesworth, 1723–5.

Collins, Thomas, *Brief Reflections suggested to those inhabitants of the City of Coventry who patronized the Procession in Spon street, July 8, 1844*. Coventry, 1844.

The Coventry Corpus Christi Plays, ed. Pamela M. King and Clifford Davidson. Kalamazoo: Medieval Institute Publications, 2000.

The Coventry Leet Book, ed. M. D. Harris, 2 vols., EETS os 146. 1907 and 1913; repr. New York: Kraus, 1971.

Davies, Rowland, *Journal of the Very Reverend Rowland Davies*, ed. Richard Caulfield. London: Camden Society, 1857.

de Rapin-Thoyras, Paul, *Histoire d'Angleterre*, vol. i. La Haye: A. de Rogissart, 1724.

Defoe, Daniel, *A Tour Thro' the Whole Island of Great Britain*, 2 vols. 1724–7; repr. London: Peter Davies, 1927.

Deloney, Thomas, *Coventry made free by Godina, countess of Chester. To the tune of, Prince Arthur died at Ludlow, &c.* London: [Broadsheet], ca. 1750.

Deloney, Thomas, *Garland of Good Will*. London: G. Conyers, ca. 1700.

Deloney, Thomas, *The Works of Thomas Deloney*, ed. F. O. Mann. Oxford: Clarendon Press, 1912.

Domesday Book, ed. John Morris, 38 vols. Chichester: Phillimore, 1975–.

Drayton, Michael, *The Works of Michael Drayton*, ed. J. William Hebel, corrected edn., 5 vols. Oxford: Basil Blackwell, 1961.

Dugdale, William, *The Antiquities of Coventry*. Coventry: J. Jones, 1765.

Dugdale, William, *The Antiquities of Warwickshire*. London: T. Warren, 1656.

The Early Records of Medieval Coventry, ed. Peter Coss. London: Oxford University Press, 1986.

English Historical Documents, vol. i: *c.500–1042*, ed. Dorothy Whitelock, 2nd edn. London: Routledge, 1979.

English Historical Documents, vol. ii: *1042–1189*, ed. David C. Douglas and George W. Greenaway. New York: Oxford University Press, 1968.

Fabyan, Robert, *The New Chronicles of England and France, in two parts; by Robert Fabyan. Named by himself The Concordance of Histories. Reprinted from Pynson's edition of 1516*, ed. H. Ellis. London: F. C. & J. Rivington et al., 1811.

Faure, Raoul C., *Lady Godiva and Master Tom*. New York: Harper Brothers, 1948.

Fiennes, Celia, *Through England on a Side Saddle in the Time of William and Mary*, ed. Emily Griffiths. London: Field & Tuer, 1888.

Foxe, John, *Acts and Monuments of Martyrs*, vol. ii. London: John Day, 1583.

Fretton, William George, *Memorials of the Fullers' or Walkers' Guild, Coventry*. Coventry: Coventry Corporation, 1878.

Geisel, Theodore Seuss, *The Seven Lady Godivas*. New York: Random House, 1939.

Gifford, William, "The Etonian," *The Quarterly Review*, 25 (1821), 95–112.

Grafton, Richard, *Grafton's Chronicle; or, History of England*, ed. Henry Ellis. London: J. Johnson, 1809.

Hans Engelska Fru, produced by Oscar Hemberg. Isepa-Wengeroff Productions, 1927.

Hardyng, John, *The Chronicle of John Hardyng . . . Together with the Continuation by Richard Grafton*, ed. Henry Ellis. London: F. C. and J. Rivington etc., 1812.

Hawkes, H. W., *A Brief History of the Earl of Mercia, Lady Godiva, and Peeping Tom of Coventry . . . Accompanied with an Original Poem on the Lady Riding Through the Town*, 7th edn. Coventry: Rollason, 1838(?).

Hemingi Chartularium Ecclesiae Wigorniensis, ed. T. Hearne, vol. i. Oxford: Sheldonian Theatre, 1723.

Henry, Archdeacon of Huntington, *Historia Anglorum; The History of the English People*. Oxford: Clarendon Press, 1996.

Henry of Huntington, *Henrici Archidiaconi Huntendunensis Historia Anglorum*, ed. Thomas Arnold. London: Longman et al., 1879.

Higden, Ralph, *Polychronicon Ranulphi Higden Monachi Cestrensis*, ed. Joseph Lumby, vol. vii: *1865–86*. London: Longman, Green, 1865–86; repr. New York: Kraus, 1964.

The History of Coventry Show Fair with an account of Lady Godiva and Peeping Tom, and a description of the Grand Procession, new edn., with engravings. Coventry: Henry Merridew, 1843(?).

Holinshed, Ralph, *Chronicles of England, Scotland, and Ireland*, 6 vols., vol. i. London: J. Johnson et al., 1807.

The Holy Bible (Douai and Rheims). Baltimore: John Murphy, 1914.

A Hundred Merry Tales and other English Jest-books of the Fifteenth and Sixteenth Centuries, ed. P. M. Zall. Lincoln: University of Nebraska Press, 1963.

Hunt, Leigh, *Indicator*. London, 1822.

Hunt, Leigh, *Poetical Works of Leigh Hunt*, ed. H. S. Milford. London: Oxford University Press, 1923.

Hunt, Leigh, *Tales by Leigh Hunt*, ed. William Knight. London: Patterson, 1891.

Ingram, R. W., ed., *Coventry, Records of Early English Drama*. Toronto: Toronto University Press, 1981.

Ingulph, *The Chronicle of Croyland Abbey by Ingulph*, ed. W. de Gray Birch. Wisbech: Leach & Son, 1883.

Jago, Richard, "Edge-Hill," in *The Works of the English Poets*, ed. Alexander Chalmers, vol. xvii. London: J. Johnson, 1810.

John of Fordun, *Johannis de Fordun Scotichronicon Genuinum*, ed. Thomas Hearnes, vol. v. Oxford: Sheldonian Theatre, 1722.

John of Worcester, *The Chronicle of John of Worcester*, trans. Jennifer Bray and P. McGurk, ed. R. R. Darlington and P. McGurk, vol. ii. Oxford: Clarendon Press, 1995.

Kingsley, Charles, *Hereward the Wake*, 2 vols. 1866; New York: J. F. Taylor, 1898.

Korda, Alexander, and Sidney Gilliat, *Lady Godiva Rides Again*. London: British Film Institute, 1951.

Landor, Walter Savage, *Imaginary Conversations of Literary Men and Statesmen*, vol. ii. London: James Duncan, 1829.

Lives of Edward the Confessor, ed. H. R. Luard. London: Longman et al., 1858.

Longfellow, Henry W., "Journal," MS Am 1340 (184) 1829–30. Cambridge, Mass., Harvard University Houghton Library.

The Mabinogi, ed. and trans. Patrick Ford. Berkeley: University of California Press, 1977.

Maeterlinck, M., *Monna Vanna*. Paris: Charpentier-Fasquelle, 1924.

Marks, Leo, *Peeping Tom*. London: Faber & Faber, 1998.

"Maxims I," in *The Exeter Book*, ed. G. P. Krapp and E. V. K. Dobbie, Anglo-Saxon Poetic Records 3. New York: Columbia University Press, 1937.

Mell, Max, "Lady Godiva," in *Die drei Grazien des Traumes. Fünf Novellen*. Leipzig: Insel-Verlag, 1906.

Moravia, Alberto, *Lady Godiva and Other Stories*, trans. Angus Davidson. London: Secker & Warburg, 1975.

Moultrie, John [pseud. G.M.], "Godiva – A Tale," *The Etonian*, 2 (1820), 149–62.

Napier, A. S., "An Old English Vision of Leofric Earl of Mercia," *Transactions of the Philological Society 1907–10*, 2 (1910), 180–7.

O'Keeffe, John, *Peeping Tom; or the Coventry Magistrates: A Comic Opera in Two Acts*. New York: Addison B. Price, 1813.

Orderic Vitalis, *The Ecclesiastical History of Orderic Vitalis*, ed. Marjorie Chibnall, vol. ii. Oxford: Clarendon Press, 1968.

The Oxford Book of Medieval Latin Verse, ed. F. J. E. Raby. Oxford: Clarendon Press, 1959.

Paris, Matthew, *Chronica Majora*, ed. H. L. Luard, Rolls Series, 7 vols. London: Longman, 1872–84.

Paris, Matthew, *La Estoire de Seint Aedward le Rei attributed to Matthew Paris*, ed. Kathryn Young Wallace. London: Anglo-Norman Text Society, 1983.

Paris, Matthew, *Flores Historiarum*, ed. H. L. Luard, Rolls Series, 3 vols., vol. i. London: HMSO, 1890.

Paris, Matthew, *The Flowers of History*, trans. C. D. Yonge, 2 vols., vol. i. London: Henry G. Bohn, 1853.

Plath, Sylvia, *Ariel*. New York: Harper & Row, 1966.

A Relation of A Short Survey of Twenty-Six Counties Observed in a seven weeks Journey begun on August 11, 1634 by a Captain, a Lieutenant, and an Ancient, ed. L. G. Wickham Legg. London: F. E. Robinson, 1904.

Roger of Wendover, *Chronica sive Flores Historiarum*, ed. H. O. Coxe, 5 vols., vol. i. London: English Historical Society, 1841–4.

Roger of Wendover, *Flowers of History*, trans. J. A. Giles, vol. i. London: Henry G. Bohn, 1849.

Sweet's Anglo-Saxon Reader, in Prose and Verse, ed. Dorothy Whitelock, 15th edn.

Oxford: Clarendon Press, 1975.

Talfourd, Francis, and W. P. Hale, *Godiva; or, Ye Ladye of Coventrie and ye Exyle Fayrie*. London: H. Lacy, 1851.

Tavel, Ronald, "The Life of Lady Godiva: An Hysterical Drama," in *The New Underground Theatre*, ed. R. J. Schroeder. New York: Bantam, 1968.

Tennyson, Alfred, *The Poems of Tennyson*, ed. Christopher Ricks, vol. ii. London: Longman, 1987.

"Text of the Warwickshire Domesday," ed. and trans. W. F. Carter, in *The Victoria History of the County of Warwick*, ed. H. A. Doubleday and William Page, vol. i. London: Archibald Constable, 1904.

The Towneley Plays, ed. Martin Stevens and A. C. Cawley, 2 vols., vol. i. Oxford: Oxford University Press, 1994.

Two Coventry Corpus Christi Plays, ed. Craig Hardin, 2nd edn. London: Oxford University Press, 1957.

Two of the Saxon Chronicles Parallel: With Supplementary Extracts from the Others, ed. Charles Plummer, rev. edn. Oxford: Clarendon Press, 1952.

Voragine, Jacobus de, *The Golden Legend*, trans. William Granger Ryan, 2 vols. Princeton: Princeton University Press, 1993.

Walter of Coventry, *Memoriale Fratris Walteri de Coventria*, ed. William Stubbs, vol. i. London: Longman, 1872.

William of Malmesbury, *Gesta Pontificum Anglorum*, ed. N. E. S. A. Hamilton, Rolls Series 52. 1870; repr. Wiesbaden: Kraus, 1964.

William of Malmesbury, *Gesta Regum Anglorum; The History of the English Kings*, ed. and trans. R. A. B. Mynors, completed by R. M. Thomson and M. Winterbottom, 2 vols., vol. i. Oxford: Clarendon Press, 1998.

Wolcot, John, "The Convention Bill; Ode to Mr. Pitt," in *The Works of Peter Pindar*. London: Walker & Edwards, 1816.

Wordsworth, William, *The Critical Opinions of William Wordsworth*, ed. M. L. Peacock. Baltimore: Johns Hopkins University Press, 1950.

Secondary Sources

Baldwin, Frances E., *Sumptuary Legislation and Personal Regulation in England*. Baltimore: Johns Hopkins University Press, 1926.

Bartlett, Robert, *England under the Norman and Angevin Kings*, New Oxford History of England, ed. J. M. Roberts. Oxford: Clarendon Press, 2000.

Beckwith, Sarah, *Christ's Body: Identity, Culture and Society in Late Medieval Writings*. London and New York: Routledge, 1993.

Beckwith, Sarah, "Making the World in York and the York Cycle," in Sarah Kay and Miri Rubin, eds., *Framing Medieval Bodies*, pp. 254–76. Manchester: Manchester University Press, 1994.

Beckwith, Sarah, *Signifying God: Social Relation and Symbolic Act in the York Corpus*

Christi Plays. Chicago: University of Chicago Press, 2001.

Beech, George, "England and Aquitaine in the Century before the Norman Conquest," *Anglo-Saxon England*, 19 (1990), 81–102.

Berger, John, et al., *Ways of Seeing*. New York: Viking, 1972.

Blair, Peter Hunter, *An Introduction to Anglo-Saxon England*. Cambridge: Cambridge University Press, 1956.

Blau, Herbert, *Nothing in Itself: Complexions of Fashions*. Bloomington: Indiana University Press, 1999.

Bolton, Diane K., "The Legend of Lady Godiva," in W. B. Stephens, ed., *A History of the County of Warwick*, vol. viii: *The City of Coventry and Borough of Warwick*, pp. 242–7. London: Institute of Historical Research, 1969.

Brett, Martin, "John of Worcester and his Contemporaries," in R. H. C. Davis and J. M. Wallace-Hadrill, eds., *The Writing of History in the Middle Ages*, pp. 101–26. Oxford: Clarendon Press, 1981.

Brooke, C., *From Alfred to Henry III: 871–1272*. New York: Norton, 1961.

Buckley, Jerome H., *Tennyson: The Growth of a Poet*. Cambridge, Mass.: Harvard University Press, 1960.

Burbidge, F. Bliss, *Old Coventry and Lady Godiva*. Birmingham: Cornish Brothers, 1952.

Campbell, James, "Some Twelfth-Century Views of the Anglo-Saxon Past," *Peritia*, 3 (1984), 131–50.

Campbell, James, ed., *The Anglo-Saxons*. Ithaca: Cornell University Press, 1982.

Cantor, Norman, *Inventing the Middle Ages*. New York: William Morrow, 1991.

Christ, Carol, "The Feminine Spirit in Victorian Poetry," *English Literary History*, 54 (1987), 385–401.

Clark, Kenneth, *The Nude: A Study in Ideal Form*. New York: Doubleday, 1956.

Clarke, Peter, *The English Nobility under Edward the Confessor*, Oxford Historical Monographs. Oxford: Clarendon Press, 1994.

Clarke, Ronald Aquilla, and Patrick A. E. Day, *Lady Godiva: Images of a Legend in Art and Society*. Coventry: City of Coventry Leisure Services, 1982.

Clover, Carol, *Men, Women, and Chain Saws: Gender in the Modern Horror Film*. Princeton: Princeton University Press, 1992.

Conway, M. D., "Lady Godiva at Home," *Harper's Monthly Magazine* (1866), 625–33.

Coss, Peter, *Lordship, Knighthood and Locality: A Study in English Society c.1180–c.1280*. Cambridge: Cambridge University Press, 1991.

Crary, Jonathan, *Techniques of the Observer: On Vision and Modernity in the Nineteenth Century*. Cambridge, Mass.: MIT Press, 1990.

Culler, Dwight A., *The Poetry of Tennyson*. New Haven: Yale University Press, 1977.

Daniell, David, *William Tyndale: A Biography*. New Haven: Yale University Press, 1994.

Davidson, H. R. Ellis, "The Ride: In Folk Tradition," in Joan C. Lancaster, ed., *Godiva of Coventry*, Coventry Papers 1, pp. 61–73. Coventry: Coventry Corporation, 1967.

Davis, R. H. C., *The Early History of Coventry*, Dugdale Society Occasional Papers 24. Oxford: Dugdale Society, 1976.

DeMott, Robert, "Cathy Ames and Lady Godiva: A Contribution to *East of Eden*'s Background," *Steinbeck Quarterly*, 14 (1981), 72–83.

Dickens, A. G., *The English Reformation*. New York: Schocken, 1969.

Doane, Mary Ann, "The 'Woman's Film': Possession and Address," in M. A. Doane, P. Mellencamp, and L. Williams, eds., *Re-Vision: Essays in Feminist Film Criticism*, American Film Institute Monograph Series 5. Frederick, Md.: University Publications of America, 1984.

Donoghue, Daniel, "Lady Godiva," in Donald Scragg and Carol Weinberg, eds., *Literary Appropriations of the Anglo-Saxons from the Thirteenth to the Twentieth Century*, pp. 194–214. Cambridge: Cambridge University Press, 2000.

Duby, Georges, *A History of Private Life: Revelations of the Medieval World*, trans. Arthur Goldhammer, ed. Philippe Ariès and Georges Duby, vol. ii. Cambridge, Mass.: Belknap, 1988.

Duffy, Eamon, *The Stripping of the Altars*. New Haven: Yale University Press, 1992.

Eco, Umberto, "Dreaming of the Middle Ages," trans. William Weaver, in *Faith in Fakes*, pp. 61–72. London: Secker & Warburg, 1986.

Eco, Umberto, "Living in the New Middle Ages," trans. William Weaver, in *Faith in Fakes*, pp. 73–85. London: Secker & Warburg, 1986.

Egan, Susanna, "Glad Rags for Lady Godiva: Woman's Story as Womanstance in Elizabeth Barrett Browning's *Aurora Leigh*," *English Studies in Canada*, 20 (1994), 283–300.

Eidson, John Olin, *Tennyson in America: His Reputation and Influence*. Athens, GA: University of Georgia Press, 1943.

Ellis, John, *Visible Fictions: Cinema; Television; Video*. London: Routledge & Kegan Paul, 1982.

Farmer, David Hugh, *The Oxford Dictionary of Saints*. Oxford: Oxford University Press, 1978.

Fell, Christine, "A 'friwif locbore' Revisited," *Anglo-Saxon England*, 13 (1984), 157–65.

Fell, Christine, *Women in Anglo-Saxon England*. Oxford: Basil Blackwell, 1986.

Fenichel, Otto, "The Scopophilic Instinct and Identification," *The International Journal of Psycho-Analysis*, 18 (1937), 6–34.

Ferguson, Sarah, with Benita Stoney, *Victoria and Albert: Life at Osborne House*. London: Weidenfeld & Nicolson, 1991.

Fleming, Robin, *Kings and Lords in Conquest England*, Cambridge Studies in Medieval Life and Thought, 4th series, 15. Cambridge: Cambridge University Press, 1991.

Freeman, Edward A., *History of the Norman Conquest*, rev. American edn., 6 vols., vol. ii. Oxford: Clarendon Press, 1873.

Freeman, Edward A., *Old English History for Children*. London: Macmillan, 1869.

French, Katherine L., "The Legend of Lady Godiva and the Image of the Female Body," *Journal of Medieval History*, 18 (1992), 3–20.

Freud, Sigmund, *Instincts and their Vicissitudes*, in *Standard Edition of the Complete Psychological Works of Sigmund Freud: On the History of the Psycho-Analytic Movement; Papers on Metapsychology; and Other Works*, vol. xiv: *1914–16*, ed. James Strachey, pp. 117–40. London: Hogarth Press and the Institute of Psycho-Analysis, 1953–74.

Freud, Sigmund, "The Psycho-Analytic View of Psychogenic Disturbance of Vision," from *Five Lectures on Psycho-Analysis*, in *Standard Edition of the Complete Psychological Works of Sigmund Freud: Five Lectures on Psycho-Analysis; Leonardo da Vinci; and Other Works*, vol. xi: *1910*, ed. James Strachey, pp. 211–18. London: Hogarth Press and the Institute of Psycho-Analysis, 1953–74.

Freud, Sigmund, "The Sexual Aberrations," from *Three Essays on the Theory of Sexuality*, in *Standard Edition of the Complete Psychological Works of Sigmund Freud: The Case of Hysteria; Three Essays on Sexuality; and Other Works*, vol. vii: *1901–05*, ed. James Strachey, pp. 135–72. London: Hogarth Press and the Institute of Psycho-Analysis, 1953–74.

Frida, Emil Bohuslav, [*Legendy*]: *Sv. Vojtech, Godiva, Armida, Trilogie or Simsonovi*. Soubor dramatickych spisu 7. V Praze: Rodina, 1935.

Galloway, Andrew, "Writing History in England," in David Wallace, ed., *The Cambridge History of Medieval English History*. Cambridge: Cambridge University Press, 1999.

Garber, Marjorie B., *Vested Interests: Cross-Dressing and Cultural Anxiety*. New York: Routledge/Chapman & Hall, 1992.

Gardiner, H. C., *Mysteries' End*. 1946; repr. Hamden, Conn.: Archon, 1967.

Gillingham, John, "Henry of Huntingdon and the English Nation," in S. Forde, L. Johnson, and A. V. Murray, eds., *Concepts of National Identity in the Middle Ages*, Leeds Texts and Monographs, NS 14, pp. 75–101. Leeds: University of Leeds Press, 1995.

Gooder, Arthur, and Eileen Gooder, "Coventry before 1355: Unity or Division?" *Midland History*, 6 (1981), 1–38.

Gordon, Alexander, "Godiva," in Leslie Stephen and Sidney Lee, eds., *Dictionary of National Biography*. London: Oxford University Press, 1921–2.

Gover, J. E. B., A. Mawer, and F. M. Stenton, *The Place Names of Warwickshire*. English Place-Name Society 13. Cambridge: Cambridge University Press, 1936.

Gransden, Antonia, *Historical Writing in England, c.550–c.1307*, vol. i. London: Routledge & Kegan Paul, 1974.

Graves, Robert, *The White Goddess*. New York: Farrar, Straus & Cudahy, 1948.

Green, Judith, *The Aristocracy of Norman England*. Cambridge: Cambridge University Press, 1997.

Häfele, Karl, *Die Godivasage und ihre Behandlung in der Literatur*, ed. J. Hoops, Anglistische Forschungen. Heidelberg: Winter, 1929.

Harris, Mary Dormer, *Life in an Old English Town*, Social England series. London: Swan Sonnenschein, 1898.

Hartland, E. S., "Peeping Tom and Lady Godiva," *Folk-Lore*, 1 (1890), 207–26.

Helgerson, R., *Forms of Nationhood in the Elizabethan Writings of England*. Chicago: University of Chicago Press, 1992.

Heslop, T. A., "The Production of *de luxe* Manuscripts and the Patronage of King Cnut and Queen Emma," *Anglo-Saxon England*, 19 (1990), 151–95.

Hickling, W., *History and Antiquities of the City of Coventry, being a Descriptive Guide to its Public Buildings, Institutions, Antiquities, &c. also the Ancient Legend of Lady Godiva. The Whole Compiled from the Earliest Authentic Records, and Continued to the Present Time*. Coventry: W. Hickling, 1846.

Hill, D., *An Atlas of Anglo-Saxon England*. Toronto: University of Toronto Press, 1981.

The History of British Rock, 4: *The British Invasion*. Audio CD. San Diego, 1988.

Hollander, Anne, *Seeing Through Clothes*. Berkeley: University of California Press, 1978.

Hollander, Anne, *Sex and Suits*. New York: Knopf, 1994.

Hough, Richard, *Victoria and Albert*. New York: St. Martin's, 1996.

Hunt, Alan, *Governance of the Consuming Passions: A History of Sumptuary Law*. New York: St. Martin's, 1996.

Hunt, Lynn, "Introduction: Obscenity and the Origins of Modernity, 1500–1800," in Lynn Hunt, ed., *The Invention of Pornography: Obscenity and the Origins of Modernity*, pp. 9–45. New York: Zone, 1993.

Hunt, W., "Matthew Paris," in *Dictionary of National Biography*, pp. 152–4. London: Oxford University Press, 1921–2.

James, Mervyn, "Ritual, Drama and Social Body in the Late Medieval English Town," *Past and Present*, 98 (1983), 3–29.

Jenkyns, Richard, *Dignity and Decadence: Victorian Art and the Classical Inheritance*. London: HarperCollins, 1991.

Jewell, Helen, *Women in Medieval England*. Manchester: Manchester University Press, 1996.

John, Eric, "The End of Anglo-Saxon England," in James Campbell, ed., *The Anglo-Saxons*. Ithaca: Cornell University Press, 1982.

Johnston, Alexandra F., "'All the World was a Stage': Records of Early English Drama," in Eckehard Simon, ed., *The Theatre of Medieval Europe: New Research in Early Drama*, pp. 117–29. Cambridge: Cambridge University Press, 1991.

Jump, John D., ed., *Tennyson: The Critical Heritage*. London: Routledge & Kegan Paul, 1967.

Kaplan, E. Ann, "Is the Gaze Male?" in her *Women in Film: Both Sides of the Camera*, pp. 23–35. New York and London: Routledge, 1983.

Karras, Ruth Mazo, *Common Women: Prostitution and Sexuality in Medieval England*. Oxford and New York: Oxford University Press, 1996.

Ker, N. R., *Catalogue of Manuscripts Containing Anglo-Saxon; reprinted with a supplement*. 1957; repr. Oxford: Clarendon Press, 1977.

Kinvig, R. H., "Warwickshire," in H. C. Darby, ed., *The Domesday Geography of Midland England*, 2nd edn., pp. 273–312. Cambridge: Cambridge University

Press, 1971.

Kirby, H. T., "In Memory of Lady Godiva," *Country Life*, 21 Oct. 1949, pp. 1214–15.

Kobialka, Michal, *This is my Body: Representational Practices in the Early Middle Ages*. Ann Arbor: University of Michigan Press, 1999.

Kolve, V. A., *The Play Called Corpus Christi*. Stanford: Stanford University Press, 1966.

Lancaster, Joan, "The City of Coventry: Introduction," in W. B. Stephens, ed., *A History of the County of Warwick*, vol. viii: *The City of Coventry and Borough of Warwick*, pp. 1–10. London: Oxford University Press, 1969.

Lancaster, Joan C., "The Coventry Forged Charters: A Reconsideration," *Bulletin of the Institute of Historical Research*, 27 (1954), 113–40.

Lancaster, Joan C., *Godiva of Coventry*, Coventry Papers 1. Coventry: Coventry Corporation, 1967.

Langdon-Davies, John, *Lady Godiva: The Future of Nakedness*. New York: Harper, 1928.

Lennie, Campbell, *Landseer: The Victorian Paragon*. London: Hamish Hamilton, 1976.

Liebrecht, Felix, *Zur Volkskunde: Alte und Neue Aufsatze*. Heilbronn: Henninger, 1879.

Lindenbaum, Sheila, "Ceremony and Oligarchy: The London Midsummer Watch," in Barbara A. Hanawalt and Kathryn L. Reyerson, eds., *City and Spectacle in Medieval Europe*, Medieval Studies at Minnesota 6, pp. 171–88. Minneapolis: University of Minnesota Press, 1994.

Loyn, H. R., *Anglo-Saxon England and the Norman Conquest*. London: Longman, 1962.

Loyn, H. R., *The Governance of Anglo-Saxon England, 500–1087*. Stanford: Stanford University Press, 1984.

Mac Cana, Proinsias, *Celtic Mythology*, rev. edn. Feltham, UK: Newnes, 1983.

Magennis, Hugh, "'No Sex Please, We're Anglo-Saxons'? Attitudes to Sexuality in Old English Prose and Poetry," *Leeds Studies in English*, 26 (1995), 1–27.

Marsh, Joss, "Spectacle," in Herbert F. Tucker, ed., *A Companion to Victorian Literature and Culture*, pp. 276–88. Oxford: Blackwell, 1999.

Mayne, Judith, "The Woman at the Keyhole: Women's Cinema and Feminist Criticism," in M. A. Doane, P. Mellencamp, and L. Williams, eds., *Re-Vision: Essays in Feminist Film Criticism*, American Film Institute Monograph Series 5, pp. 49–66. Frederick, Md.: University Publications of America, 1984.

McRee, Benjamin R., "Unity or Division? The Social Meaning of Guild Ceremony in Urban Communities," in Barbara A. Hanawalt and Kathryn L. Reyerson, eds., *City and Spectacle in Medieval Europe*, Medieval Studies at Minnesota 6, pp. 189–207. Minneapolis: University of Minnesota Press, 1994.

Mermin, Dorothy, *Godiva's Ride*. Bloomington: Indiana University Press, 1993.

Miles, Margaret, *Carnal Knowing: Female Nakedness and Religious Meaning in the Christian West*. Boston: Beacon Press, 1989.

Morgan, Judith, and Neil Morgan, *Dr. Seuss and Mr. Geisel*. New York: Random House, 1995.

Mulvey, Laura, "Afterthoughts on 'Visual Pleasure and Narrative Cinema' Inspired by King Vidor's *Duel in the Sun* (1946)," in her *Visual and Other Pleasures*, pp. 29–38. Theories of Representation and Difference, ed. Teresa de Lauretis. Bloomington: Indiana University Press, 1989.

Mulvey, Laura, "Visual Pleasure and Narrative Cinema," in her *Visual and Other Pleasures*. Theories of Representation and Difference, ed. Teresa de Lauretis. Bloomington: Indiana University Press, 1989.

Nelson, Alan H., *The Medieval English Stage: Corpus Christi Pageants and Plays*. Chicago: University of Chicago Press, 1974.

Owen-Crocker, Gale R., *Dress in Anglo-Saxon England*. Manchester: Manchester University Press, 1986.

Page, R. I., *Life in Anglo-Saxon England*, English Life Series, ed. Peter Quennell. London: B. T. Batsford, 1970.

Partner, Nancy F., *Serious Entertainments: The Writing of History in Twelfth Century England*. Chicago: University of Chicago Press, 1977.

Phythian-Adams, Charles, "Ceremony and the Citizen: The Communal Year at Coventry, 1450–1550," in Peter Clark and Paul Slack, eds., *Crisis and Order in English Towns, 1500–1700*, pp. 57–85. London: Routledge & Kegan Paul, 1972.

Phythian-Adams, Charles, *Desolation of a City: Coventry and the Urban Crisis of the Late Middle Ages*, Past and Present Publications, ed. T. H. Aston. Cambridge: Cambridge University Press, 1979.

Poole, B., *Coventry: Its History and Antiquities*. London: John Russell Smith, 1870.

Reader, William, *New Coventry Guide . . . The Origin and Description of the Coventry Show Fair and Peeping Tom*. Coventry: Rollason and Reader, 1824(?).

Richardson, Joanna, *Victoria and Albert*. New York: Quadrangle, 1977.

Rivas, Manuel Linares, *Lady Godiva: Leyenda historica ec cuatro jornadas en verso*. Madrid: Nuevo Mundo, 1912.

Round, J. H., "Introduction to the Warwickshire Domesday," in *The Victoria History of the County of Warwick*, ed. H. A. Doubleday and William Page, vol. i, pp. 269–97. London: Archibald Constable, 1904.

Rubin, Miri, *Corpus Christi: The Eucharist in Late Medieval Culture*. Cambridge: Cambridge University Press, 1991.

Ruskin, John, *Sesame and Lilies*. Boston: Ginn & Co., 1927.

Sartre, J.-P., *Being and Nothingness*, trans. Hazel E. Barnes. New York: Philosophical Library, 1956.

Shannon, E. S., *Tennyson and the Reviewers: A Study of his Literary Reputation and the Influence of the Critics upon his Poetry 1827–1851*. Cambridge, Mass.: Harvard University Press, 1952.

Sharp, Thomas, *A Dissertation on the Pageants or Dramatic Mysteries Anciently Performed at Coventry*. Coventry: Merridew, 1825.

Shaw, George Bernard, "The Living Pictures," *Saturday Review*, 6 Apr. 1895, pp. 443–5.

Shippey, T. A., "The Undeveloped Image: Anglo-Saxon in Popular Consciousness from Turner to Tolkien," in Donald Scragg and Carole Weinberg, eds., *Literary Appropriations of the Anglo-Saxons from the Thirteenth to the Twentieth Century*, pp. 215–36. Cambridge: Cambridge University Press, 2000.

Smith, Alison, *Exposed: The Victorian Nude*. New York: Watson-Guptill, 2002.

Smith, Alison, *The Victorian Nude*. Manchester: Manchester University Press, 1996.

Solomon-Godeau, Abigail, "The Legs of the Countess," in Emily Apter and William Pietz, eds., *Fetishism as Cultural Discourse*, pp. 266–306. Ithaca and London: Cornell University Press, 1993.

Sowden, Lewis, *Lady of Coventry*. London: Robert Hale, 1950.

Spearing, A. C., *The Medieval Poet as Voyeur: Looking and Listening in Medieval Love-Narratives*. Cambridge: Cambridge University Press, 1993.

Stafford, P., *Queen Emma and Queen Edith*. Oxford: Blackwell, 1997.

Stafford, Pauline, "Women in Domesday," *Reading Medieval Studies*, 15 (1989), 75–94.

Stafford, Pauline, "Women and the Norman Conquest," *Transactions of the Royal Historical Society*, 6th series, 4, pp. 221–50. London: Royal Historical Society, 1994.

Stallybrass, Peter, "Transvestism and the 'Body Beneath': Speculating on the Boy Actor," in Susan Zimmerman, ed., *Erotic Politics: Desire on the Renaissance Stage*, pp. 64–83. New York: Routledge, 1992.

Stanbury, Sarah, "The Virgin's Gaze: Spectacle and Transgression in Middle English Lyrics of the Passion," *Proceedings of the Modern Language Association*, 106 (1991), 1083–93.

Stanbury, Sarah, "The Voyeur and the Private Life in *Troilus and Criseyde*," *Studies in the Age of Chaucer*, 13 (1991), 141–58.

Steele, Valerie, *Fetish: Fashion, Sex, and Power*. New York: Oxford University Press, 1996.

Stenton, F. M., *Anglo-Saxon England*, 3rd edn. Oxford and New York: Oxford University Press, 1971.

Stenton, F. M., "The Historical Bearing of Place-Name Studies: The Place of Women in Anglo-Saxon Society," in D. M. Stenton, ed., *Preparatory to Anglo-Saxon England*, pp. 314–24. Oxford: Clarendon Press, 1970.

Stephen, Leslie, and Sidney Lee, eds., *Dictionary of National Biography*, 22 vols. London: Humphrey Milford, 1917–22.

Stephens, F. G., *Sir Edwin Landseer*. London: Sampson, 1881.

Stephens, W. B., ed., *A History of the County of Warwick*, vol. viii: *The City of Coventry and Borough of Warwick*. London: Institute for Historical Research, 1969.

Strong, Roy, *The Cult of Elizabeth: Elizabethan Portraiture and Pageantry*. London: Thames & Hudson, 1977.

Stubbs, Charles William, *Historical Memorials of Ely Cathedral*. New York: Scribner's, 1897.

Symonds, John Addington, *Wine, Women and Song: Medieval Latin Students' Songs*.

London: Chatto & Windus, 1907.

Tait, James, *The Medieval English Borough*. Manchester: Manchester University Press, 1936.

Van Dyne, Susan R., *Revising Life: Sylvia Plath's Ariel Poems*. Chapel Hill: University of North Carolina Press, 1993.

Vaughan, Richard, *Matthew Paris*. Cambridge: Cambridge University Press, 1958.

Vaughan, Richard, *Chronicles of Matthew Paris*. Gloucester: Alan Sutton, 1984.

Wainwright, F. T., "Æthelflæd, Lady of the Mercians," in P. Clemoes, ed., *The Anglo-Saxons*, pp. 53–70. London: Bowes & Bowes, 1959.

Walkowitz, Judith, *Prostitution and Victorian Society*. Cambridge: Cambridge University Press, 1980.

Waterton, C., *Wanderings in South America*, ed. J. G. Wood. London, 1879.

Waterton, E., "Hereward le Wake: The Countess Lucy," *Notes and Queries*, 6th series, 6 (1882), 30–1.

Weintraub, Stanley, *Victoria: An Intimate Biography*. New York: Truman Talley/ E. P. Dutton, 1987.

Williams, Linda, "When the Woman Looks," in Mary Ann Doane, Patricia Mellencamp, and Linda Williams, eds., *Re-Vision: Essays on Feminist Film Criticism*, American Film Institute Monograph Series 5, pp. 83–99. Frederick, Md.: University Publications of America, 1984.

Woolner, Amy, *Thomas Woolner R.A., Sculptor and Poet: His Life in Letters*. New York: Dutton, 1917.

Zika, Charles, "Hosts, Processions and Pilgrimages: Controlling the Sacred in Fifteenth-Century Germany," *Past and Present*, 118 (1988), 25–64.

Index

Page numbers for plates are indicated in **bold**.